KU-223-401

A2 Economics
UNIT 6

Edexcel

Unit 6: The UK in the Global Economy

Russell Dudley-Smith

Philip Allan Updates
Market Place
Deddington
Oxfordshire
OX15 0SE

tel: 01869 338652
fax: 01869 337590
e-mail: sales@philipallan.co.uk
www.philipallan.co.uk

This Guide has been written specifically to support students preparing for the Edexcel A2 Economics Unit 6 examination. The content has been neither approved nor endorsed by Edexcel and remains the sole responsibility of the author.

Printed by Information Press, Eynsham, Oxford

Contents

Introduction

■ ■ ■

Content Guidance

■ ■ ■

Questions and Answers

Introduction

Aims

This guide has been written to prepare students for Unit 6 of Edexcel's A-level (A2) GCE examinations in economics. It provides an overview of the knowledge and skills required to achieve a high grade in the examination for The UK in the Global Economy. This unit's main emphasis is on international economics.

However, this is also the synoptic paper of the A-level: candidates will have opportunities to introduce material from their work in all the other units. The questions are designed to allow candidates to develop microeconomic as well as macroeconomic perspectives. The official specification for Unit 6 contains a large number of overlapping and slightly fragmented topics — this guide aims to condense these to make learning easier. A good approach would be for you to organise your notes in line with the following eight main topics presented in this guide:

(1) Public expenditure and taxation: fiscal issues; the pros and cons of different kinds of tax; the changing size and composition of government spending; reasons for changes in the size of public sector borrowing; the implications of differences in the fiscal positions of countries (even this section of the specification has an international flavour).

(2) Macroeconomic policy: the use of monetary and fiscal policies in targeting the level of aggregate demand; a comparison with supply-side policies (there is a clear link here to the specification for Unit 3); application of the AD/AS model in an international context; the potential *conflict* between macroeconomic objectives; using the model to analyse the impact of external shocks to the UK and world economy — for example, the consequences of higher oil prices.

(3) Unemployment and inflation: the Phillips curve and Friedman's critique of the use of the curve for policy purposes; the concept of the non-accelerating inflation rate of unemployment (NAIRU) and the natural rate of output; recent trends in inflation and unemployment; their causes and costs in an international context.

(4) The balance of payments and exchange rates: the main components of the balance of payments; the causes of balance of payments disequilibrium; policies designed to remedy such disequilibrium; the possible conflict between this and other macroeconomic objectives; how exchange rates are determined; the pros and cons of fixed vs floating exchange rates; the use of exchange rates as an instrument of policy.

(5) International competitiveness: measures of international competitiveness and the factors affecting the UK's competitiveness with its trading partners; policies designed to increase competitiveness.

(6) European Monetary Union: costs and benefits of monetary union; the implications for macroeconomic policy of joining or staying outside the euro-zone; the controversy surrounding the Stability Pact.

(7) International trade: the importance of international trade; trade liberalisation and protectionism, including the use of tariffs, quotas and non-tariff barriers to trade;

the difference between free trade areas and customs unions; the impact of trading blocs and the possible conflict with the aims of the World Trade Organisation (WTO).

(8) Globalisation: the growing economic interdependence of economies; the significance of capital mobility; the impact of technological innovations such as the internet; the role of multinational companies (MNCs) in globalisation; the significance of inward foreign investment to the UK.

How to use this guide

The experience of the first Unit 6 examination in the summer of 2002 suggests that candidates can find the synoptic and evaluative demands of the unit quite difficult. This guide aims to make these requirements clear and suggests many ways in which you can meet them. A central focus is on exam technique. The guide includes typical questions and answers, and explains what the examiners are looking for. Common mistakes are highlighted and strategies for increasing marks are suggested. The guide should be used as a supplement to a taught course along with textbooks and other materials that your teachers recommend.

This introduction explains the examination format and the skills that will be tested. It provides useful tips on revision planning and sitting the examination. A 4-week revision programme for Unit 6 is also included.

The Content Guidance section provides an overview of the eight main topics, identifying what has to be learnt and explaining the theoretical requirements of the unit. There is an emphasis on the links back to previous units and the importance of the evaluation component at A2.

The final part of the guide provides questions and answers on the economic concepts and topics in Unit 6. There are three essay questions and three data-response questions covering the main topic areas, with a selection of student answers to give you an idea of the level of answer required to achieve a grade A. A few grade-C answers are included for you to see what can go wrong under timed conditions. The answers include examiner's comments, which are a helpful way of getting to know the expectations of those who will mark your papers. After reviewing the Unit 6 topics, you should have a go at these example questions, *ideally under timed conditions*, and then compare your work with the answers and comments provided. This will identify areas of weakness that require further work.

Exam format

Unit 6 makes up 40% of the total marks for A2 (20% of the total A-level). It is worth a maximum of 120 Uniform Mark Scheme (UMS) marks. The exam has two sections. Section A is made up of three essay questions, each in two parts. Candidates must answer one of these questions. The essays are marked out of 100 and the candidate's score is then divided by two to give a mark out of 50. In section B there is a choice between two data-response questions, again worth 50 marks. Both sections are therefore of equal worth, with a maximum raw mark of 100.

As a rough guide to the standards required, for the June 2002 examinations the grade-A boundary was set at 60/100, grade C at 46/100 and grade E at 34/100. However, these grade thresholds change according to the examiners' perception of the quality of the candidates and the difficulty of the papers.

The amount of time allowed for the examination is 1 hour and 45 minutes. It is sensible to allocate 5 minutes for reading through the essay questions and writing a quick plan of your answer. You should spend no more than 45 minutes writing the essay itself. This will then allow a further 5 minutes to read through the data-response questions and 45 minutes to write your answers. Finally, you should spend a further 5 minutes checking through all your work at the end.

Assessment objectives

There are four assessment objectives, or sets of skills, in each unit of AS and A-level economics. When questions are set, these skills are very much in the minds of the examiners. The objectives are *knowledge, application, analysis* and *evaluation*. These are defined in the following table. You should note that the analysis and evaluation components have a higher weighting than at AS.

Objective	Assessment objectives	A2 weighting
1	**Knowledge and understanding:** demonstrate knowledge and understanding of the specified content.	20%
2	**Application:** apply knowledge and critical understanding to problems and issues arising from both familiar and unfamiliar situations.	20%
3	**Analysis:** analyse economic problems and issues.	30%
4	**Evaluation:** evaluate economic arguments and evidence, making informed judgements.	30%

When questions are set, a great deal of thought is put into the choice of *command words*. These are the directive words in each question, such as *define, explain* and *discuss*. It is vital that you understand the intention behind the command words because they signal different levels of expected response. As the questions at the end of this guide make clear, you can lose many marks if you disregard the command word.

Knowledge and understanding

The command words for this assessment objective include: *define, outline* and *distinguish between*. For example, in Unit 6 you are expected to be able to define terms such as real exchange rate, NAIRU, competitiveness and direct inward investment. You are also expected to be able to show basic knowledge of institutional arrangements such as the World Trade Organisation (WTO) and the Monetary Policy Committee (MPC). Finally, you should be able to demonstrate that you understand the economic models that you are expected to apply in the examination.

Application and analysis

These assessment objectives are indicated by command words such as *analyse* and *explain*. Often the best way of answering such questions is to draw a diagram based on relevant economic theory. The idea here is for you to show that you can apply international economics to the real-world case studies presented in the data-response questions. Typical analysis questions in this unit draw upon the AD/AS model, macroeconomic linkages (e.g. the effect of a recession in one country on the performance of another), potential conflicts between objectives (e.g. the controversy surrounding the Phillips curve) and the theory of protectionism (e.g. the welfare effect of a tariff).

Evaluation

This is the assessment objective most often ignored by candidates, but it carries a large proportion of the total marks available. Command words include: *examine*, *evaluate*, *discuss*, *assess*, *comment upon* and *to what extent*. Any of these words in a question show that examiners expect candidates to demonstrate some critical understanding of the issues being discussed. Strategies for gaining evaluation marks include discussing the pros and cons of an argument, assessing the use of evidence presented in the passage, drawing out the wider context of the discussion, and coming to a well-thought-out conclusion. For example, a question that begins 'Examine the factors that determine...' does not simply require a list of factors, but needs some attempt to argue which are the most important. If you simply produce a bullet-point list of factors as your answer, you will automatically lose a substantial number of the marks available.

Planning your revision: general points

Effective revision relies on you learning the material systematically. For this reason, you should survey the material for the entire unit well before you sit down to do your final revision. For the June exam, start revising during the Easter holidays when you should:

- **Check that you have covered all elements of the specification.** This can be freely downloaded from the Edexcel website at **www.edexcel.org.uk**. The best version is in the 'Teachers' Guide' because it includes extended advice about the specification requirement.
- **Get your notes in order.** A good approach is to write out each *row* of the specification as the 'contents' page for each section of your notes — you may want to use the eight topic sections described in this guide as the basis for your file sections. Check that you have notes for each section. If you are in any doubt about which section your notes should be filed under, ask your teacher for help.
- **Think about how you might be able to add value to your answers.** Unit 6 is the only module that requires you to write essays. By far the easiest way for you to score high marks in essays is to bring in material from extra reading. In the area of international economics, there are two or three relevant articles every week in *The Economist* and many others in the financial pages of newspapers. Make a habit of reading and making notes on these articles — and putting these notes in the relevant topic section of your file. A good approach is to read the article and, without looking at the text, to write a summary of the main themes discussed.

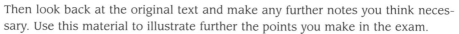

Then look back at the original text and make any further notes you think necessary. Use this material to illustrate further the points you make in the exam.

- **Do not cut out topics from your revision.** Each data-response question in this unit is likely to contain questions drawn from several of the specification topics. It is not safe to ignore some topics because you are pressed for time. You must plan to cover the entire range of subjects. This is manageable if you allocate your time sensibly.

- **Begin to learn your notes systematically.** It is important that you adopt a method of committing summaries of your notes to memory. Merely reading them through whilst listening to music and drinking a cup of coffee is not going to get you very far — though, dangerously, it will feel like you have been revising. Everyone has a different method of learning things by heart. However, as a *minimum*, you must reduce your material to condensed lists of points. You should aim to be able to reproduce these lists by heart by the end of the Easter holiday. The only way that you can be sure that you have achieved this is by testing yourself by writing out the lists, having put the originals away.

- **Make use of your friends.** An excellent way of reinforcing learning is to discuss particular topics with friends. Try to teach a part of the specification to someone you know who is also taking the examination and get him or her to do the same for you.

- **Practise questions under timed conditions.** It is important that you test yourself under pressure of time. If you have not done any timed work in school, make sure you are given the opportunity to do so. Use some of the questions at the back of this guide for extra practice.

A 4-week structured revision plan

Day	Week 1	Week 2	Week 3	Week 4
One	Taxation. Pros and cons of different kinds of tax.	The AD/AS model. Impact of shocks such as higher oil prices.	Inflation and unemployment: causes and consequences.	Protectionism: tariffs, quotas and non-tariff barriers to trade.
Two	Government spending: changing patterns and consequences.	Monetary policy: interest rates and the role of the Monetary Policy Committee.	The Phillips curve. Friedman's analysis. The NAIRU.	The role of, and potential conflict between, trading blocs and the WTO.
Three	Reasons for changes in the size of public sector borrowing.	Conflicts between macroeconomic objectives in the AD/AS model.	Balance of payments: components, disequilibrium.	Globalisation (1): economic inter-dependence between countries.
Four	Evaluation of the Stability Pact of the EU and its consequences for the UK.	Supply-side policies: comparison with demand-side policies.	Exchange rate regimes and EMU. Measures of international competitiveness.	Globalisation (2): the role of multinational companies.
Five	Exam practice: do the first essay question from this guide.	Exam practice: do the first data-response question from this guide.	Exam practice: do the second and third essay questions from this guide.	Exam practice: do the second and third data-response questions from this guide.

introduction

For final revision in the weeks leading up to the examination, you should relearn the material, with an emphasis on trying to gain a complete knowledge of your notes. If you work efficiently, this should not take very long — say half an hour a day for each unit. It is better to do a small amount of revision each day than to try to learn the whole course just before the exam. It is unlikely that more intensive revision than this will be very productive.

How to answer essay questions

You will have had some experience of writing longer responses in Unit 3. In Unit 6, however, you have to write a full 45-minute essay split into only two parts — usually for either 40 and 60 marks, or with both sections worth 50 (remember that the total is divided by two to give a total mark out of 50, equal to the data-response). It makes sense to divide your time according to the marks for each section: for example, 18 minutes and 27 minutes respectively for an essay offering 40 marks for section (a) and 60 marks for section (b).

In the summer 2002 paper, all the essay sections were evaluative, beginning with keywords such as *examine*, *assess* and *evaluate*. It is therefore imperative that you adopt a critical approach for all essay sections. Avoid the temptation to reel off all you know about a subject without structuring your answer according to the question set. Be sure to come to an evaluative conclusion at the end.

Further tips for the essay questions are:
- **Plan your answer.** Write down your main points for answering both sections (no more than one-word paragraph headings) before you begin your answer. This should increase the clarity of your answer and will also prevent you from starting a question and then finding that you cannot answer part (b).
- **Use microeconomics and macroeconomics wherever possible.** Remember that this is a synoptic unit. You are expected to use the full range of economic theory that you have covered across the six modules. The most impressive answers are those that discuss both micro- and macroeconomic perspectives.
- **Draw diagrams wherever possible.** These need to be labelled clearly and key areas or points indicated. The AD/AS framework is at the heart of international macroeconomics, so use it in your analysis of exogenous shocks. On the micro-economic front, a diagram showing the welfare effect of a tariff or quota is very useful in discussing issues of protectionism. It is rare for questions to ask you to draw diagrams, *but you are likely to score high marks for using them*.
- **Be strict with your time allocation for each question.** Too many candidates write at enormous length on the essay section and then have to leave sections of the data-response question unanswered because of a shortage of time. This is a partic-ular problem with the synoptic unit because you will have a lot to write. Remember that the law of diminishing returns applies to answering individual sections.
- **Do not get trapped by unexpected parts of a question.** Candidates often report that they were disconcerted by an unfamiliar expression or set of data. One way to prevent this is to think carefully before making your choice of question. It is

much better to choose a question where you have something to say about all the parts than one where you can only do some of the parts, however well. If you do get stuck, don't waste time trying to puzzle out the unfamiliar, but instead write down some basic definitions and leave the question behind. If you have time, you can always come back to it at the end of the examination.

- **Pick up on the economic jargon terms in the question.** These will almost always be worth defining in your explanation. Do include relevant background knowledge in your answer.
- **Practise writing under timed conditions.** Organising your thoughts to write an essay under timed conditions is an advanced skill. This can only be acquired through practice. Start by writing some essays that you have considered beforehand, then move on to some unseen questions. This advice is particularly important for Unit 6 because you are likely to need some essay-writing experience before you are up to full speed for the exam.
- **Highlight your evaluative material.** Make clear to the examiner where you have attempted to gain evaluation marks. You can do this by starting a sentence or paragraph with, for example, 'However' or 'On the other hand' or 'Nonetheless, it is possible to criticise this point of view'. Make sure that you do not use the same indicator phrase for each of your evaluative paragraphs.
- **Come to a conclusion.** Each section of your essay should contain a formal conclusion, summing up the arguments put forward in the rest of the essay. A good place to start is to draw together the paragraph headings in your plan. It is then essential that you write a formal conclusion stating, for example, which of the arguments carries the most weight or what further evidence would be needed to decide the matter. It is perfectly acceptable (and often the most intelligent response) to be a little tentative: economics is not an exact science.

A further tip for answering essay questions is to address the words *in the question* in your introduction. This will put you on a proper evaluative footing from the start. Do not be content with simply defining the words in the question. Try to highlight a critical issue or theme for the rest of the essay.

How to answer data-response questions

There is a choice between two data-response questions in Unit 6. It is important to check through each question to make sure that there are no sections that you cannot answer. For example, if you have forgotten what supply-side policies are, do not try to answer a question that has 10 marks for a discussion of them.

The data-response questions for Unit 6 tend to come from newspaper and magazine articles. It is therefore a good idea to get into the habit of reading a broadsheet newspaper or *The Economist* and asking yourself whether the articles would make good Unit 6 questions. A useful exercise is to write your own question paper and mark scheme for a particular article and ask your teacher to comment.

You should be up to date in your knowledge of the main trends in the economy at the time of the examination and for the previous 5 years or so. You should also have a good understanding of the UK policy framework and some knowledge of international current affairs, especially the changing nature of the EU.

There are a number of rules of thumb to follow when answering data-response questions:

- **Identify the economic theory behind the question.** Questions tend to be set with economic theory in mind. If at all possible, use the relevant theory rather than writing a general answer. Do not hesitate to use theoretical diagrams and economic terms in your answer. These may need to be either micro or macro diagrams. For example, when discussing issues of macroeconomic policy use AD/AS diagrams, and when analysing factors affecting exchange rate changes use supply and demand diagrams.
- **Answers should always be related to the context provided.** You need to apply the theory to the context. Purely theoretical answers are unlikely to score high marks.
- **Do not take key terms in the questions for granted.** Some strong candidates have a tendency to drop marks because they forget to include basic definitions. You may know what a term means but you have to persuade the examiner that this is the case. Be sure that you can define all the key terms outlined in the Content Guidance section of this guide.
- **Make use of the text or data provided.** If the question says 'with reference to the passage', you *must* use brief quotations from the passage to support your answer. Very often, the text will provide you with at least enough to make a good start to a question. On the other hand, there is little point to answers that merely copy out large sections of the text provided, so make sure you avoid this pitfall.
- **Look carefully at the scale of graphs or bar charts.** The units of measurement matter — many candidates make mistakes in this area. For example, do not confuse rates of growth with levels of GDP or inflation rates with price levels.
- **Identify trends in data, not just levels.** If you are asked to describe data or are using them as evidence, then calculate percentage changes over the relevant time scale rather than just listing values.
- **Move beyond the confines of the data.** Unless the question specifically directs you to discuss only issues referred to in the data, you should widen the discussion as much as possible. Very often, sections towards the end of each question allow a more general level of response. Use material from other case studies you have looked at and arguments or issues not included in the passage.
- **Be critical of the data provided.** The arguments put forward in the passage are not correct just because they appear in an examination paper. Every author makes a *selection* of evidence and arguments. It is always possible to put forward another point of view even if it is only a matter of a different emphasis. There are many marks available for candidates who demonstrate that they are capable of achieving a degree of critical distance from the material provided.
- **Allocate time sensibly.** You have no more than approximately 45 minutes for the data-response question. Remember that it is much easier to score marks at the

beginning of an answer than at the end. Do not spend so much time on the first few questions that you have to leave the last questions unanswered. Be sensible, too, about the time you spend on each section: 2-mark questions require much shorter answers than 10-mark questions.

- **Do not be distracted by 10-mark sections.** You only have 45 minutes: that is, slightly less than 1 minute per mark. You are not expected to write an essay for 10 marks. The examiners understand that time is limited. They also understand that it is only possible to write a couple of paragraphs in 9 or 10 minutes.
- **Keep up to date.** There are articles on international economics every week in broadsheet newspapers. Get into the habit of reading some and keeping track of developments in the world economy. This means that your answers will be much better informed.
- **Pay particular attention to key words.** One of the problems of doing a data-response question in timed conditions is that the key words change with each question. One moment you are writing elementary definitions and the next some critical evaluation is required. It is vital that you keep up with these shifts of expectation. Some examples include:

Define — make clear the meaning of a term. You should make a list of all the terms in the specification and commit the definitions to memory. It is often worth providing an illustrative example to back up a definition.

Analyse — explain the economic logic behind a situation. Often the use of a diagram is helpful here.

Using a diagram — these need to be presented clearly. Many candidates draw their diagrams too small — a third of a side is not unreasonable. Label the axes. If you have equilibrium points to indicate, dot down or across to the axes and label these values. If your diagram is showing a move from one equilibrium to another, draw arrows along the axes to show the changes. If your diagram goes wrong, put a single line through it and start again. Under no circumstances should you submit a diagram with some of the lines on it crossed out.

Examine, evaluate, discuss, assess, to what extent — these are evaluation key words. They are directing you to examine critically the matter at hand. A good strategy is to rehearse the pros and cons of the arguments concerned. You should appraise the balance of argument and indicate which points have the greatest or least significance. For evaluation sections with a high number of marks, you should come to a conclusion at the end of your answer.

Grade descriptions

Edexcel provides official grade descriptions for examiners to use as a guide to their marking. The grade you achieve will depend on the extent to which you have met the four assessment objectives described on pp. 6–7. However, you do not have to give perfect answers to achieve a grade A. The examiners are very much aware that you are under considerable time pressure when you do these units and Unit 6 is no exception. There is a great deal to do and there is no way that you will be able to cover every aspect of a question during the exam.

Do not panic if you know you have got part of a question wrong, because it is still possible to achieve a high grade. Shortcomings in some aspects of your examination answers may be balanced by better performance elsewhere.

The author's comments are in *italics* after the official grade descriptions listed below.

Grade A

Candidates will demonstrate in-depth knowledge and critical understanding of a wide range of economic theories and concepts. They will apply this knowledge and understanding to analyse familiar and unfamiliar situations, issues and problems using appropriate numerical and non-numerical techniques accurately. They will evaluate evidence and arguments effectively, making reasoned judgements to present appropriate and well-supported conclusions.

In practice, two things distinguish grade-A candidates. The first is a thorough knowledge of the basic specification so that there are few, if any, blank sections in their answers. The second is an ability to evaluate — the last sentence of the official description is the most important.

Grade C

Candidates will demonstrate knowledge and understanding of a limited range of economic theories and concepts. They will show some ability to use this knowledge and understanding in order to analyse familiar and unfamiliar situations, issues and problems making use of numerical and non-numerical techniques. Candidates' evaluation of evidence and arguments will be limited.

Grade-C candidates tend to have a good basic knowledge of only some parts of the specification. They tend to leave some sections unanswered and to make only limited use of the data and passage provided. They pay very little attention to the meaning of key words and tend to ignore commands to evaluate.

Content
Guidance

This section focuses on essential information, including economic concepts and models that students need to understand for Unit 6: The UK in the Global Economy (Synoptic Unit). These are explained under the following headings:

- Public expenditure and taxation (p. 17)
- Macroeconomic policy in an international context (p. 23)
- Unemployment and inflation, and the Phillips curve debate (p. 30)
- The balance of payments and exchange rate determination (p. 34)
- International competitiveness (p. 38)
- European monetary union (p. 41)
- International trade and protectionism (p. 44)
- Globalisation and multinational investment (p. 49)

Public expenditure and taxation

The Unit 6 specification requires you to have a more extensive knowledge of both the theory and practice of fiscal policy than the introductory material of Unit 3. Note that the term *fiscal policy* refers to any attempt to manage the economy through changes in government spending or taxation. It is important that you try to apply the ideas presented in this guide to the current fiscal situation: for example, by studying the most recent Budget statement (available on **www.hm-treasury.gov.uk**). You should develop some understanding of the composition of both taxation and government spending. Fiscal regimes centred on goals such as the 'golden rule' will need to be evaluated, and the causes and consequences of fiscal changes should be understood.

Different types of tax

UK governments have traditionally raised revenue through a wide range of taxes.
- **Direct taxes** are those raised on income. Examples are income tax (on the income of private individuals) and corporation tax (on the profits of companies).
- **Indirect taxes** are those levied on expenditure. An example is value added tax (VAT) charged on most goods at 17.5%.

The variety of taxes levied makes the UK tax system complex, and reduces the transparency of the overall level of taxation. The table below shows the Treasury's forecast for income from various taxes during the fiscal year 2002/03.

Tax	Revenue (£bn)
Income tax	114
National insurance	66
VAT	64
Excise duties	38
Corporation tax	29
Business rates	18
Council tax	17
Others (e.g. stamp duty)	54
Total	**400**

A useful way of evaluating the different types of tax is to consider the following issues:
- **Equity.** This refers to the impact of the tax on people at different levels of income. Consider whether each tax is *regressive* (where the tax paid falls as a proportion of income for those on higher incomes) or *progressive* (where tax rises as a proportion of income for those on higher incomes). For example, the UK income tax structure is progressive because the stepped marginal rates of tax (10%, 22%, 40%) ensure a rising *average* rate of tax as income rises.

- **Efficiency.** Direct taxes have been criticised for reducing incentives to work. On the other hand, indirect taxes tend to raise prices above marginal costs, creating allocative inefficiency. Even when a tax is imposed on a good involving negative externalities, it is easy for government to raise the rate well above the social optimum. The material on market and government failure from Unit 2 should be used when considering these issues.
- **Ease of collection.** Some taxes are easier to evade or more costly to collect than others. Most workers in the UK are on PAYE: their employers pay their income tax direct to the Inland Revenue. However, the unofficial economy escapes these arrangements — there are estimates that this may amount to as much as 15% of GDP. Indirect taxes, such as VAT, impose a considerable burden of red tape because companies have to keep their accounts in an approved form.

The composition of government expenditure

The level of government involvement in the economy has grown significantly in recent decades. A major distinction needs to be drawn between the following:

- **Transfer payments** where income is taken from one person in tax and given to another as benefits. Examples include the Jobseeker's Allowance and disability benefit.
- **General government spending** on goods and services. Examples are building new motorways, paying the wages of teachers and nurses, and defence expenditure.

The table below shows the major components of government spending in the fiscal year 2002/03.

Item of expenditure	Amount (£bn)
Social security	117
National Health Service	66
Education	54
Defence	24
Law and order	23
Debt interest	20
Housing and environment	19
Industry, agriculture and employment	17
Transport	12
Other expenditure	67
Total	**419**

An effective method of evaluating the composition of government spending is to consider the economic rationale for the government getting involved in these areas in the first place. Again, the Unit 2 concepts of merit goods, public goods and negative externalities should be used here.

- **Redistribution of income.** This is a major reason for government expenditure and goes some way to explain the very high figure for social security in the table. Expenditure on the benefit system, affordable housing and the provision of some health care free at the point of use all protect the most vulnerable members of society. However, there may be a cost to the economy in terms of reduced incentives from high levels of tax.

- **Provision of merit goods.** Merit goods are goods that people may undervalue in a free market, such as education. However, the *level* of provision of merit goods is difficult to determine because, by definition, there can be no market guidelines. You should also be aware that the concept is controversial: can governments really know individual long-term preferences better than the individuals themselves?
- **Provision of public goods.** Public goods are goods that are non-excludable and non-reducible in consumption, and which cannot be provided by market forces, such as nuclear defence. However, this line of argument may also serve to legitimise the provision of some 'public bads'.
- **Dealing with negative externalities.** An example is the provision of public transport to ease road congestion and its associated pollution. Again, just because *some* expenditure in these areas is necessary does not guarantee that *all* expenditure will be worthwhile. The opportunity costs need to be considered.

All of these forms of intervention can result in **government failure** as resources get misallocated. Thus, much of the debate on government expenditure focuses on the potential for waste created by such high levels of spending.

Over the past decade, the level of government spending has risen sharply in real terms. These increases will accelerate with the plans outlined in the July 2002 *Spending Review*, which programmed an extra £63bn of expenditure, three-quarters of which has been allocated to education and health. A number of factors explain the changing size and composition of this expenditure:

- **Political control of government expenditure.** The control of government expenditure, unlike that of monetary policy, remains in the political sphere. Cutting government spending is virtually impossible in politically sensitive areas (except as improvements in efficiency). This creates a 'ratchet' effect, where spending in most areas can rise, or stay constant, but not fall.
- **The increasing payments of benefits to the poor.** This is redistributive, but also perhaps a way of appeasing groups marginalised by capitalism.
- **The high income elasticity of demand** for some government expenditure, such as health service provision and education. As real GDP has grown, the demand for these goods has risen even faster.
- **The decline of traditional respect for authority**, requiring greater expenditure on policing.
- **Global insecurity.** The 'peace dividend' from the demise of the Soviet Union is now rapidly being spent on increased defence against new threats from abroad.

Public sector borrowing

The excess of government spending over tax revenue is known as the **fiscal deficit** (and also as the **public sector deficit**). In the past, the Treasury has also called this item the **public sector borrowing requirement** (PSBR) and the public sector net cash requirement (PSNCR). Both of these are equivalent to the term 'fiscal deficit'. If tax revenue exceeds government spending, there is a **fiscal surplus**. A fiscal deficit implies that the government must borrow to cover its expenditure, usually by selling gilts in the open market. This incurs an interest and repayment liability for the future.

The graph below shows recent changes in the fiscal deficit together with Treasury forecasts for the future. The fiscal surpluses of the late 1990s have evaporated, leaving the UK with a forecast £20bn deficit for 2002/03.

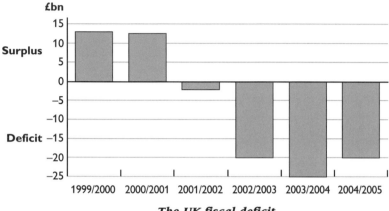

The UK fiscal deficit

An analysis of the *causes* of these changes to the fiscal position should include the following:

- **The business cycle.** In periods of strong economic growth, tax revenues are buoyant. Employment and therefore incomes rise, generating higher levels of direct tax revenue. Consumption also increases, raising the indirect tax take. During the downturn in the business cycle, tax revenues fall and government spending in areas such as unemployment benefits start rising. With the downturn in the world economy and forecast growth in UK GDP at only 1.6% for 2002/03, which is well below trend, it is not surprising to see a rise in the fiscal deficit.
- **Difficulties in controlling growth in government spending.** The demands for extra expenditure on health and education have raised the *structural* level of spending, i.e. spending independent of the state of the business cycle. This is the 'ratchet effect' referred to above.
- **The desire for low tax rates.** The government is committed to leaving income tax rates unchanged. Although business taxes and some 'stealth' taxes have increased, these do not match the extra spending plans.
- **The one-off nature of some government revenue.** Sales of mobile phone licences generated enormous revenue for the government. However, this was a windfall, not a sustainable source of government income.

An analysis of the *consequences* of these changes should include the following:

- The high **real** burden of debt that the government is faced with. In previous decades, the debt incurred by having a high public sector deficit was rapidly eroded by inflation. But independently controlled monetary policy makes this much less likely now.

- The likely impact on the level of **future** government spending and taxation. Further increases in spending will be difficult if the level of borrowing is already high.
- The **risk of inflation** if aggregate demand is raised by a large budget deficit (or even the possibility that the government will print money if the deficit gets too large to finance by selling bonds).
- The likelihood that any cuts in taxes will be seen as **temporary** if the public finances are in deficit, and so may fail to stimulate the economy. High levels of borrowing can therefore reduce the effectiveness of fiscal demand management.

Automatic vs discretionary fiscal policy

There are two basic kinds of fiscal intervention:

- **Automatic fiscal policy** refers to changes in tax revenue and government spending brought about by cyclical changes in GDP. For example, government spending automatically rises during a recession through the payment of unemployment benefits. This is an example of an **automatic stabiliser**: the extra expenditure boosts aggregate demand and so dampens the recession.
- **Discretionary fiscal policy** refers to active demand management by the government. The Chancellor of the Exchequer may, for example, decide to raise taxes during an upturn in the economy to reduce the risk of inflation.

It is possible for governments to establish fixed rules for the conduct of fiscal policy. For example, Gordon Brown adopted the '**golden rule**' shortly after the Labour government came to power in 1997. The rule states that government borrowing should, on average through the business cycle, not exceed that amount required to finance public sector net investment. The advantage of this rule is that it provides a framework for fiscal discipline and so should promote business confidence. Yet at the same time it should allow automatic stabilisers to dampen the business cycle.

Examination skills and concepts

- Being able to distinguish between the causes and consequences of changes in the fiscal position.
- Demonstrating synoptic skills by linking the ideas of market failure in Unit 2 to the need for various types of government expenditure and taxation.
- Understanding the difference between automatic and discretionary fiscal policy, and relating this to the size of the fiscal deficit.
- Being able to evaluate the use of fixed-rule fiscal regimes such as the 'golden rule'.
- Being able to interpret data on fiscal policy and to assess the consequences for the UK of imbalances in the fiscal position of its major trading partners.

Common examination errors

- Making unwarranted assumptions. For example, an increase in government spending does not in itself mean that the government will raise taxes. It is equally possible that the government will raise its level of borrowing by selling gilts (government bonds).

- Thinking that VAT is a regressive tax. In fact, VAT is not levied on many essential items, e.g. food and children's clothes. This makes its overall impact fairly proportional, although it is regressive in particular areas, such as the (lower rate) tax on household fuel.
- Failing to use the evidence provided in data-response questions. In questions that begin 'With reference to the passage…' it is essential that brief extracts are used by way of evidence. If the data are numerical, summarise any changes by calculating percentages — do not just list the numbers.
- Failing to spend enough time evaluating rather than just describing the factors causing changes to the fiscal position. A useful strategy is to provide a brief conclusion, coming to a judgement about the relative importance of the factors that you have described.

Useful exercises

- Read the financial pages of a broadsheet newspaper for a month. Look out for stories about fiscal policy. There are often articles referring to changing forecasts of public sector borrowing. Note why the forecasts have changed.
- Go to the Treasury website at **www.hm-treasury.gov.uk** and download data for the most recent fiscal year (these run from April to March). Also study the chancellor's most recent Budget speech.
- Use the internet to find data on the fiscal position of the USA and Japan. Of what significance are these data to the UK economy?
- Compare the fiscal stances of the UK and one other European country. Assess the consequences for the UK of the differences between the two countries in terms of export performance and potential membership of the euro.
- Have a discussion with a fellow student about the relative merits of fixed-rule vs discretionary fiscal regimes.
- Relate the concept of automatic stabilisers to the multiplier concept covered in Unit 3. Does the presence of multiplier processes make the conduct of fiscal policy easier or more difficult?
- Why might a balanced increase in both government spending and taxation raise the level of aggregate demand?

Linkages and common themes

Unit 6 is the **synoptic** unit in Edexcel's specification. You are expected to introduce material from all the other units in your answers. This should include both microeconomic and macroeconomic elements.

- Linkage Unit 1. It is a powerful strategy to discuss the importance of **elasticities**. For example, in analysing the distortion introduced by indirect taxes, it will be the greater the higher the price elasticity of demand concerned. The concept of **opportunity cost** is also extremely useful in a discussion of government spending.
- Linkage to Unit 2. Governments do not just provide the legal framework for markets. The UK is a mixed economy, where a great deal of expenditure is thought necessary to overcome **market failure**. Equally, a major purpose of taxation is to deal with negative externalities — hence the introduction of pollution taxes.

- Linkage to Unit 3. Fiscal policy and monetary policy are not completely independent. If the government allows a large fiscal deficit to develop, the Monetary Policy Committee may feel that the risk of inflation is higher and so raise interest rates.

Macroeconomic policy

This section of the Unit 6 specification requires you to use the AD/AS framework from Unit 3 to assess the various instruments of macroeconomic policy. The appropriateness of each policy in a variety of circumstances should be analysed. The associated problems of each approach should be understood, including the importance of time lags and the inaccuracy of much economic data about the current state of the economy. Finally, there is a strong emphasis in Unit 6 on the international context of macroeconomic policy-making.

The AD/AS model

The synoptic nature of Unit 6 means that you are expected to be able to use the macroeconomic theory of Unit 3, even though it is not mentioned explicitly in the Unit 6 specification. In the first Unit 6 examination, many candidates missed out on marks because they failed to use the AD/AS model in their macroeconomic explanations.

The main elements of the model are as follows:

- Relationships between the **price level** and the level of **real output** of the economy. Aggregate demand (AD) is total planned expenditure on goods and services produced in the UK. Aggregate supply (AS) is the total planned output of goods and services.
- The concept of a **full-employment level of output** at which all factors of production available to the country are being used. This defines the perfectly inelastic part of the short-run aggregate supply curve.
- The idea of an **equilibrium** level of output that may be below the full-employment level of output — the basic Keynesian starting-point.
- A distinction between **short-run** and **long-run** aggregate supply. In the short run, the elasticity of AS depends upon the level of spare capacity in the economy. As the economy moves closer to the boundary of the production possibility frontier (PPF), the short-run AS curve becomes more inelastic. Factors of production become scarce and firms have to raise prices to be in a position to pay higher wages and attract workers in short supply. In the long run, the PPF itself may expand with resource discoveries or technological innovations, shifting the short-run AS curve to the right.

You may have been taught many variations on this basic model. These can be useful for evaluation, but the simple model will take your analysis a long way.

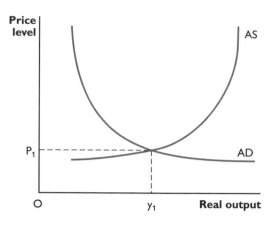

Short-run AD/AS equilibrium

The impact of shocks to the macroeconomy

The AD/AS model can be used to analyse the impact of shocks to the UK macro-economy. It is important to distinguish events that will cause a shift in aggregate demand and those that will affect aggregate supply:

- **Aggregate demand** will change if any of the components of AD changes. It is often helpful to check through the formula for AD: $C + I + G + (X - M)$. For example, the impact of an increase in government expenditure is to shift the aggregate demand curve to the right. A reduction in interest rates will have the same consequence, but this time through consumption, investment and, via a fall in the exchange rate, trade.
- **Aggregate supply** will shift if there has been a change in the productive potential of the economy. New resource discoveries, improvements in technology and gains in labour productivity are all examples of events that shift the AS curve to the right. On the other hand, wage increases or a rise in the oil price will cause a fall in AS by raising firms' costs of production.

Objectives of macroeconomic policy

There are a number of macroeconomic policy objectives:

- **Low inflation.** Rapid rises in the price level may have damaging effects on the economy. Equally, governments try to avoid a situation of deflation, where prices are actually falling.
- **Low unemployment.** Quite apart from the human consequences, workers without jobs represent lost output to the economy.
- **Balance of payments equilibrium.** A large current account deficit may not be sustainable, or may threaten sudden changes in exchange rates.
- **Steady growth.** Rising levels of real GDP are usually desired by government (although they are not an unambiguously good thing — for example, from an environmental point of view).

- **Fiscal balance.** The scope for changes in the level of government spending or taxation will be reduced if a large fiscal deficit is developing.
- **Exchange rate stability.** An unpredictable exchange rate can damage business confidence. This is particularly true for firms with large export markets.
- **Income distribution.** Governments may wish to make income distribution more equal by changing the tax and benefit system. The levels of inflation and unemployment are also important factors determining income distribution.

Instruments of macroeconomic policy

The basic distinction in discussions of macroeconomic policy is between demand management and supply-side policies. Demand-side policies include both fiscal and monetary policy.

Fiscal policy refers to any change in government spending or taxation. An increase in government spending on education or a reduction in income tax will, in the first instance, increase the level of aggregate demand. Key aspects include the following:

- A **fiscal deficit** refers to a situation where the government is spending more money than it is receiving in tax revenue.
- A deficit may be **cyclical** or **structural** in nature. A cyclical deficit occurs during a downturn in the business cycle as automatic payments increase — for example, those following an increase in unemployment — and as tax revenues decline. Cyclical deficits disappear as the economy moves into the upturn of a business cycle. A structural deficit is the underlying excess of government spending over tax revenue after cyclical components have been removed.
- The **national debt** is the sum of all borrowing by the government that has not yet been repaid. A fiscal deficit tends to increase the national debt, a fiscal surplus to reduce it because surplus funds are usually used to pay off debt early. The size of the national debt is important because the interest repayments on it can constitute a major drain on the public finances, and may reduce the scope for further changes in fiscal policy.
- Fiscal policy is conducted by the chancellor of the exchequer. In normal circumstances, fiscal changes are made annually, at the time of the **Budget**.

Monetary policy is any attempt to change the rate of interest, money supply or exchange rate. The key aspects of monetary policy include the following:

- The conduct of monetary policy is in the hands of the **Monetary Policy Committee** (MPC). The committee has the power to set interest rates independently of the wishes of government ministers. The committee meets monthly to decide whether changes in interest rates should take place.
- The government sets the MPC an **inflation target**: currently, to keep RPIX inflation within 1% either side of 2.5%. The MPC targets the RPIX rather than the RPI because the former excludes the effect on the cost of living of changes in mortgage interest repayments. This ensures that a rise in interest rates does not raise the measure of inflation that the MPC is charged with targeting. Since the committee was set up in 1997, inflation has always been inside this corridor.

Supply-side polices are aimed at increasing the productive potential of the economy (expanding the PPF). The key aspects of supply-side policies include the following:

- Measures to increase **competition**. These include deregulation of the marketplace, allowing greater competition within the private sector: for example, the deregulation of the banking industry in the 1980s, which allowed building societies to offer overdrafts to customers in the same way as banks. Another measure to increase competition is the reduction in the amount of 'red tape' that companies have to face, e.g. reforms of health and safety legislation that has been expensive to implement and changes in VAT accounting. Privatisation of public sector enterprises, such as British Telecom, aims to give them the incentive to cut costs, raise finance and improve the quality of their product. There have also been measures to increase competition in the labour market by reducing the powers of trade unions. However, each of these measures is controversial. Firms may exploit deregulation, resulting in instabilities in the economy or a loss of tax revenue to the government. And the privatisation of British Rail is hardly a good advertisement for this aspect of supply-side policies. Further, has the reduction in trade union power had an adverse effect on the distribution of income and the rights of employees?

- Policies to maintain **price stability**. These include having a fixed-rule monetary policy (the inflation target of 2.5% with an independent committee charged with sticking to it), so as to reduce inflationary expectations. Low rates of inflation may be important for the supply side, so that price signalling in markets is not disrupted by inflationary 'noise'. However, fixed-rule regimes of this kind may be too inflexible to deal with major shocks to the economy from the rest of the world.

- Policies to ensure **price flexibility**. Policies here might include the abolition of government price controls, such as minimum wages, wage ceilings, rent controls and agricultural subsidies. However, measures such as the minimum wage clearly play an important part in the redistribution of income. They may also increase labour productivity by encouraging firms to provide training to justify paying the minimum wage.

- Policies to raise the level of **human capital**. The provision of education and health services may raise the productivity of workers. However, it is easy for there to be government failure here as money spent on the wrong kinds of skill can result in a misallocation of resources.

- Policies to enhance **incentives**. The Conservative government of the early 1980s argued that a switch from direct to indirect taxes, along with a reduction in the overall tax burden, would raise incentives to work and possibly also raise the tax revenue of government. However, other economists argue for greater involvement by workers in the ownership of the companies they work for. The introduction of profit-related pay to develop a 'stakeholder' economy is often suggested.

The diagram opposite shows the successful implementation of supply-side policies, indicating the increase in real output brought about by an increase in productive potential in the economy. The falling costs of production allow higher output at lower prices.

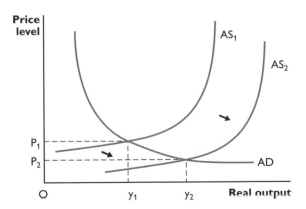

Successful implementation of supply-side policies

Policy regimes

There are two basic kinds of macroeconomic policy regime:

- **Demand management** refers to any attempt by government to control the level of aggregate demand, through either fiscal policy or monetary policy. This kind of intervention tends to be associated with Keynesian economics.
- **Endogenous growth policy** refers to the belief that, if provided with the right conditions, the economy will grow through market forces and technological improvement. The focus is then on supply-side policies to provide optimal conditions for growth. The characteristics of the new economy — a dominant service sector, outsourced part-time flexible workers and rapid computerisation — are seen as positive indicators of endogenous growth. This emphasis on the supply side, combined with neutral and fixed-rule monetary and fiscal policy, is characteristic of monetarist economists.

Dealing with the risk of deflation

In the previous diagram, a rise in aggregate supply raised output but also threatened a fall in the price level. This is a relatively benign form of deflation, easily dealt with by the Monetary Policy Committee. When rising real incomes increase confidence, reductions in interest rates, by raising aggregate demand, should ensure that inflation remains within its target zone.

However, a second form of deflation — caused by falls in aggregate demand — is more difficult to deal with, as shown in the diagram overleaf. In this case the risk is that the economy will experience falling prices *and* falling real output. The threat of this kind of deflation may reduce consumer and business confidence to such an extent that cuts in interest rates have little effect on the level of aggregate demand. This may be a reason for the government to adopt a fairly flexible fiscal policy regime within a framework of a fixed-rule monetary policy. It is one of the reasons why the UK government is currently reluctant to join the Stability and Growth Pact of the euro-zone.

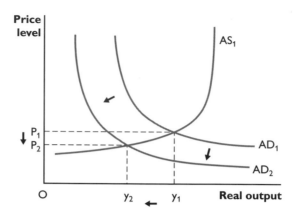

Deflation caused by falling aggregate demand

International context

- The UK is a very **open economy**. Because a relatively high proportion of UK aggregate demand is made up of foreign trade, the economy is vulnerable to shocks from the rest of the world.
- Changes in the rates of economic growth of the UK's major trading partners can therefore have a big impact on its GDP. A decline in exports is also a fall in UK aggregate demand, resulting in a multiplied contraction.
- The UK's floating exchange rate should provide some protection from recession in other countries. As their demand for our exports falls, so will their demand for sterling. This should cause the exchange rate to depreciate and thus make UK exports more competitive on world markets. However, international capital is very mobile. This means that 'hot money' flows very rapidly between countries as speculators' exchange rate expectations change. As a result, the exchange rate can move away from competitive levels for sustained periods of time.

Problems of macroeconomic policy

When discussing the likely effectiveness of macroeconomic policy, the following issues should be included:

- **Time lags.** A problem with both monetary and fiscal policy is the delay between changes in the economy and the full effect of changes in the instruments used to deal with those changes. There will be **recognition lags**: it may take several months or even a few years for the true state of the economy at a particular date to be known. There will also be **implementation lags**: for example, it is rare for a government to want to change tax rates more than once a year for fear of raising the complexity of collection. There will also be a delay between changes in policy and the full effect of those changes working through the economy. Changes in interest rates will not affect those on fixed-rate mortgages until their fixed terms expire. A rise in taxes may, initially, be met by a fall in savings rather than by a reduction in consumption.

- **Inaccurate data.** An important issue for government is that the data it uses to make macroeconomic policy decisions are often inaccurate. A lot of data are based on survey evidence, with the results taking some time to collate. The government needs to have some indication of the **output gap** in the economy: that is, the difference between actual and potential output. In the past — for example, during the 'Lawson boom' of the late 1990s — it acted on very misleading assessments of the size of this gap.

Examination skills and concepts

- Being able to use the basic AD/AS model to analyse the impact of shocks on the UK economy, e.g. oil price changes or recessions in other parts of the world.
- Being able to evaluate the relative merits of monetary, fiscal and supply-side policies to meet macroeconomic objectives.
- Being able to relate the basket of indicators used by the Monetary Policy Committee to interest rate decision-making.
- Understanding that macroeconomic policy in the UK takes place in an international context. In particular, the exchange rate adjusts to changes in interest rates very quickly, while domestic prices are rather slow to adjust. This can create an imbalance in the economy with the possibility of a loss of competitiveness and resulting falls in real output.

Common examination errors

- Failing to draw AD/AS diagrams when analysing macroeconomic events and not indicating the equilibrium price and output levels before and after the events being analysed.
- Drawing *microeconomic* demand and supply diagrams, with axis labels such as P and Q, and lines marked D and S, when the analysis required is *macroeconomic*.
- Stopping at the initial impact of a policy change. There are likely to be lagged effects, such as the operation of the multiplier, or other delays before everyone is fully affected.
- Failing to give adequate attention to the international aspects of macroeconomic policy-making. Remember the central economic fact that the UK is an open economy in a world of rapid capital mobility.

Useful exercises

- Go to the site **www.statistics.gov.uk** and draw graphs for each of the major macroeconomic objectives, covering the last 10 years. To what extent are the data cyclical?
- Download the minutes of the most recent meeting of the Monetary Policy Committee from **www.bankofengland.co.uk.** Work through the minutes, collecting a range of indicators that informed the committee's decision. Using AD/AS diagrams, illustrate the likely effect on the price level of each of the indicators you have chosen.
- Visit **www.hm-treasury.gov.uk** and download the most recent annual Fiscal Report. Of what significance is the fiscal situation to the conduct of monetary policy?

There is a very strong link between this Unit 6 topic and the whole of Unit 3. In particular, note the following:

- It is worth downloading the Edexcel Unit 3 web guide at **www.edexcel.org.uk** and using this as the starting-point for your Unit 6 revision.
- The section 'Conflicts between objectives' in Unit 3 has been moved to the Unit 6 specification. Some of these conflicts are covered in the section on the Phillips curve below, but you should be able to discuss others, such as the effect of rapid economic growth on the current account of the balance of payments.
- There is a much greater need in Unit 6 for you to know the applied details of fiscal policy. It is important that you study, for example, some figures for recent trends in the fiscal deficit, the level of government spending and the composition of taxation.

Unemployment and inflation

Until the early 1960s there appeared to be a stable and inverse relationship between unemployment and inflation in the UK economy. This is known as the **Phillips curve**, named after the economist who discovered the relationship. Phillips plotted a curve between money-wage growth and the percentage rate of unemployment between 1861 and 1957, and found an inverse, but non-linear fit. If productivity grows at a stable rate, this relationship translates into one between inflation and unemployment because firms tend to mark up prices to cover higher unit labour costs (see the diagram below).

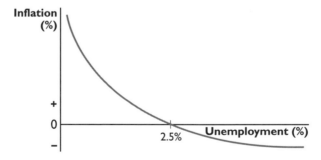

The Phillips curve

The theory behind the curve is that a rise in aggregate demand will, other things remaining equal, raise the level of output. As the economy moves towards the boundary of the PPF, this will put pressure on scarce resources such as labour. Wage rates will be forced up as firms compete for workers. Firms will tend to pass on these higher costs by marking up higher prices. Thus, as unemployment falls, the rate of inflation rises. In the original Phillips curve, 0% inflation was consistent with about 2.5% unemployment.

A number of points need to be highlighted:

- The Phillips curve suggests that the government has a **policy choice**. It can target either low rates of inflation or low rates of unemployment, but not both. Indeed, this was the basis of demand management policies in the 1960s. The Phillips curve suggests that conflict between the objectives of low inflation and low unemployment is an economic 'fact of life'.
- The analysis is **short run**. Rising wages force prices up because the economy is near the boundary of the PPF.
- Firms' mark-up of prices in the face of higher costs is typical of oligopolistic markets. This fits the Phillips curve analysis into a Keynesian framework.

The breakdown of the Phillips curve

The simple inverse relationship between unemployment and inflation broke down in the early 1970s, illustrating Goodhart's Law that 'any perceived statistical regularity tends to break down as soon as it is adopted for policy purposes'! Dramatic increases in inflation were accompanied by little change in the level of unemployment. Worse, the deflationary policies thought necessary to eliminate double-digit inflation led to very large increases in unemployment.

Milton Friedman, whose analysis rested on the idea of **adaptive expectations**, had predicted this breakdown in the curve. Suppose that initially people have low inflationary expectations and the government boosts the level of aggregate demand by printing money. In the short run this may lead some people to think that their real income has increased, so raising the level of real output and reducing the level of unemployment. However, gradually people will begin to realise that the boom was artificially induced by government. Prices will rise and people will increase their inflationary expectations. For governments to 'fool' people a second time will require *higher than predicted* increases in expenditure and, with a lag, *accelerating* inflation. In the long run, for Friedman, the Phillips curve is therefore vertical.

Friedman's analysis suggested the existence of a **natural rate** of output, determined by markets and the supply side of the economy, at which people would have zero inflationary expectations. This corresponds to the **non-accelerating-inflation rate of unemployment (NAIRU)**. The analysis also suggests the existence of a long-run perfectly inelastic AS curve (but one that can shift, not through demand-side but through supply-side policies or through endogenous growth).

An important aspect of Friedman's analysis is that people learn from their mistakes. The faster the 'adaptation', the less useful are the short-run surprises. In other words, the more the original Phillips curve is used for policy, the more quickly it breaks down. Friedman also warned that, should a government be foolish enough to take an economy up the vertical long-run AS curve by printing money, the damage done as inflation disrupted market signals would shift the curve to the right and raise the natural rate of unemployment.

Causes of unemployment and inflation

The causes of *unemployment* include the following:

- **Insufficient aggregate demand**, resulting in the equilibrium level of output falling below the full-employment level of output.
- **Frictional unemployment**: this refers to people who are between jobs.
- **Structural shifts** in the economy — people are without jobs in one sector of the economy even though there are vacancies in another sector. This may be because of skill gaps or other forms of labour immobility.
- **Supply-side failures.** If markets are distorted or rigid, or if there is inflationary noise disrupting price signalling, then the AS curve will shift to the left and the NAIRU will rise.

The causes of *inflation* include the following:

- **Excess aggregate demand.** This is the main focus of the Monetary Policy Committee's concern. For example, in 2002 house prices were rising by up to 20% a year. The Monetary Policy Committee considered that the resulting increase in wealth was likely to increase consumption and thus inflation. As a result, it decided not to reduce interest rates despite below-trend levels of growth.
- **Monetary growth.** Countries where the government has failed to control the growth of the money supply, such as Russia in the early 1990s, have seen very rapid increases in inflation.
- **A rise in costs**: for example, the UK has recently been hit by large public sector wage demands. Other cost pressures are often due to increases in oil and other input prices.

Recent trends in unemployment and inflation

The UK has experienced a steady fall in the level of unemployment since the mid-1990s, accompanied by a remarkably low and stable inflation rate. At the same time, the level of *employment* continued to grow, reaching record levels in 2002. A number of explanations have been put forward to explain this fall:

- The role of the **Monetary Policy Committee** in keeping inflation within the target band of 1.5–3.5% since 1997. This has encouraged confidence in the economy. It is noticeable that the UK has outperformed other European economies in this respect.
- Improvements to the **supply side** of the economy. This may be because of increased labour market flexibility following the reform of trade unions in the 1980s. Another possibility is the supply-side improvement brought about by more extensive use of information technology.
- The persistently **low rate of inflation.** This allows markets to work more efficiently, so reducing the NAIRU.
- **Permanently discouraged workers.** This refers to workers who have dropped out of the unemployment figures.

- **Jobseeker's Allowance.** The rules for qualifying for the Jobseeker's Allowance have been tightened in recent years.
- **Demographic factors.** The working population has not been growing very fast in recent years.

Examination skills and concepts

- Being able to distinguish between short- and long-term relationships between inflation and unemployment.
- Being able to explain why the simple Phillips curve is unlikely to hold except in the short run.
- Understanding, and being able to examine critically, the concept of the NAIRU.
- Being able to explain recent trends in the level of UK unemployment in an EU and global context.
- Understanding the causes and consequences of changes in the rate of inflation.

Common examination errors

- Failing to distinguish between the short run and the long run in macroeconomic analysis.
- Forgetting to evaluate the NAIRU. It is, perhaps, a slightly difficult concept to pin down with any precision.
- Making too much of traditional causes of unemployment (frictional, structural etc.) and paying too little attention to the supply-side and 'new economy' factors.

Useful exercises

- Visit the government's official data website at **www.statistics.gov.uk** and download a spreadsheet of quarterly inflation and unemployment. Use Excel to construct a graph of the UK Phillips curve. Compare the performance of the 1980s with that of the 1990s.
- If inflation is 2.5% per year (the government's target), how long does it take for average prices to double? What if inflation is 5% a year?

Linkages and common themes

There is a strong link between this section of the specification and the previous section on macroeconomic policy. A useful issue to consider at this stage is whether the Monetary Policy Committee is simply concerned with achieving its inflation target, or whether it has scope also to consider the real economy: that is, the rate of real GDP growth and the level of unemployment. Although the MPC has an inflation target, the framework of monetary policy set up in 1997 allowed for 'exceptional circumstances' in which the target would not be met. In such cases, the governor of the Bank of England must write an open letter to the chancellor explaining why the committee failed to achieve the target. This gives monetary policy some leeway for dealing with exceptional events.

The balance of payments and exchange rates

Transactions between the UK and the rest of the world are recorded in the balance of payments. A useful way to think about the balance of payments is that it is an account that records purchases and sales of sterling by those making international transactions. Purchases of sterling are recorded as positive items, sales as negative ones. Since it is not possible for someone to buy a pound without someone else selling them one, the balance of payments must add up to zero. However, the overall account is made up of several subsections that have some economic significance. It is helpful to separate out two main groups of the overall balance: the **current account** and the **capital and financial account**.

The current account

The current account of the balance of payments records:
- trade in **goods**, such as cars, oil and agricultural products
- trade in **services**, such as insurance, transport and tourism
- **income flows**, such as interest on foreign bank accounts and dividends on shares held in foreign companies
- current **transfers**, such as the UK's EU membership subscriptions

The capital and financial account

You are expected to have only a brief knowledge of capital and financial account transactions. The account records financial flows such as multinational direct investment, portfolio investment in shares and bonds, as well as changes in official government foreign exchange reserves. The balance on the capital and financial account should, apart from what are sometimes sizeable errors and omissions, exactly offset the balance on the current account.

Recent trends in the UK current account

- According to the government's official record of the balance of payments, the 2002 *Pink Book*, the UK current account is nearly always in deficit. The account is heavily **cyclical**, driven by its largest component, trade in goods. As the UK economy emerges from recession, incomes rise. Consumers in the UK have a high marginal propensity to import. Their increased expenditure on foreign goods drives the current account into deficit.
- The UK's trade in goods balance has deteriorated sharply in recent years, reaching a record low of –£33.5bn in 2001. Explanations for this usually focus on the impact of the strong performance of sterling against the euro and the long-term decline of the UK's manufacturing sector. The UK is a net exporter of capital goods and

chemicals. However, it tends to be a net importer of food, cars, aircraft and other consumer goods.

- The UK is a net exporter of oil, with a surplus of £5.4bn in 2001. Because oil has a low price elasticity of demand, the current account benefits from a rise in oil prices; but the surplus is therefore vulnerable to falls in oil prices. Annual swings as large as £3bn have not been unusual in recent years, as the world oil price has fluctuated.
- The trade in services account has been positive for every year since 1966. For the last 5 years an annual surplus of over £10bn has been achieved. The UK has positive balances in financial services, insurance, business services (e.g. advertising) and computer services. However, the UK has a deficit in travel expenditure, with a –£13.8bn balance in 2001. The foot-and-mouth outbreak and, more recently, international terrorism caused significant falls in the demand for air travel to the UK.
- The income account has been positive and growing during the last decade, with a balance of £9.6bn in 2001. For most of the 1990s, UK multinationals were responsible for more direct investment overseas than foreign multinationals in the UK. The returns from this investment therefore create a positive income balance.
- The current transfers balance is generally negative, with a balance of –£7.2bn in 2001. The balance fluctuates significantly as changes are negotiated each year to UK net payments to the EU. Although the UK has to make an annual membership payment, some of this comes back in the form of subsidies in areas such as agriculture and inner-city development.

Balance of payments disequilibrium

A country is said to have a balance of payments disequilibrium if it has a structural — that is, underlying rather than merely cyclical — current account deficit. To be sustainable, such a deficit requires a surplus on the capital and financial account. Often, this can be achieved only through high interest rates to attract 'hot money' deposits. This can damage other sectors of the economy and leaves the country vulnerable to a change in sentiment by speculators.

Policy remedies for a balance of payments disequilibrium might include the following:
- **Exchange rate adjustment.** A depreciation in the exchange rate may be required to raise international competitiveness. This may be achieved by cuts in interest rates or an increase in foreign currency reserves by the Bank of England. However, this involves a loosening of monetary policy that may threaten an increase in inflation. It also makes likely a rapid outflow of 'hot money', so tending to exaggerate the downward movement of the exchange rate by removing the funding for the current account deficit.
- **Demand management.** Reducing the level of aggregate demand by tightening monetary or fiscal policy will reduce real incomes and therefore the demand for imports. The effectiveness of such a policy depends on the size of the income

elasticity of demand for imports. There is also a real price to pay in terms of lost output and rising unemployment.
- **Supply-side policies.** Supply-side improvements may raise labour productivity in the UK, so making its exports more competitive. A focus on the quality of exports may also be effective. However, such policies tend to have limited effect in the short run.

Exchange rate systems

The UK currently has a **floating exchange rate** system. The main characteristics of such a system are as follows:
- **No significant intervention** by government. The exchange rate is allowed to find its own level through market forces.
- The potential for considerable **volatility** in the exchange rate. The vast majority of transactions in sterling are speculative — the exchange rate can therefore diverge some distance from its 'fundamental' value. This tends to create uncertainty in the minds of exporters and may reduce the level of trade-related investment.
- Some potential for **automatic adjustment** of the current account. A current account deficit will force an exchange rate depreciation unless there is a capital account surplus to finance it. A depreciation of sterling raises the competitiveness of exports and of domestically produced import substitutes. In the long run, the current account should therefore improve.
- However, in the short run, the current account may actually deteriorate if the **Marshall–Lerner condition** is not satisfied. If importers and exporters have low price elasticities of demand, the rise in the price of imports will raise expenditure on imports faster than the increase in earnings from exports. Only if the price elasticity of demand for exports plus the price elasticity of demand for imports is greater than 1 will the current account improve following an exchange rate depreciation. (Note that in this condition elasticities are reported as positive numbers for downward-sloping demand curves.)

An alternative to a floating exchange rate system is a **fixed exchange rate** regime. Such a regime has the following characteristics:
- **Intervention** by the central bank to maintain a fixed value of sterling against nominated other currencies.
- A fall in **foreign exchange reserves** when the central bank buys its own currency to support its value. This can create a target for speculators if the central bank appears to be running short of reserves.
- Greater short-run stability for exporters. However, fixed exchange rates tend to be subject to periodic **devaluations** when it becomes clear that the level set is too high and that the central bank is short of reserves.

The collapse of the UK's membership of the exchange rate mechanism (ERM) in 1992 suggested that, in a world of almost **perfect capital mobility**, fixed exchange rates are very difficult to sustain.

Explaining the high value of sterling since 1996

It is generally agreed that since the mid-1990s sterling has been some way above its **purchasing power parity** rate (the rate at which the same good would be sold at the same price in the UK and abroad when expressed in a common currency). Reasons for this include the following:

- The independence of monetary policy since 1997. The ceding of interest-setting powers to the Monetary Policy Committee may have boosted market confidence in sterling by reducing inflationary expectations. In the speculative asset market for sterling, this is likely to have been the most significant factor. However, inflation rates were already very low in the mid-1990s in the period following the ERM.
- The MPC has also tended to cut interest rates more slowly than the European Central Bank and other central banks, such as the US Federal Reserve Board. This has encouraged 'hot money' flows into the UK.
- The UK economy has been relatively strong, with growth remaining much nearer trend levels than in the rest of the EU.
- The uncertainties faced by many of the economies in the euro-zone have tended to weaken the euro and thus strengthen sterling.
- The UK benefited from high levels of foreign direct investment in the late 1990s.

Examination skills and concepts

- Being able to distinguish the main components of the UK balance of payments, and being aware of the importance of the main subdivisions of the UK current account.
- Being able to explain and assess the main factors affecting changes in the principal subdivisions of the current account.
- Being aware that the balance of payments accounts are not wholly reliable. The 'errors and omissions' entry for the account in 2000 was £3.4bn.

Common examination errors

- Confusing the 'budget deficit' (the government's fiscal position) with a 'balance of payments deficit' (a deficit in the UK current account). It is surprising how often this mistake is made. Make absolutely sure that you understand the difference.
- Failing to understand the difference between current account and capital account transactions.
- Thinking that the current account is made up of only trade in goods and services.

Useful exercises

- Do a search in the Office of National Statistics website at **www.statistics.gov.uk** for the *Pink Book*. This is the official name given to the annual record of UK balance of payments data. Download Chapter 1 of the *Pink Book*.
- Using Table 1.1 from the *Pink Book*, draw graphs of changes in the main current account balances over the last 5 years.
- For each of the trends you have identified in the exercise above, suggest reasons for the changes that have taken place. The *Pink Book* contains many clues to this.
- Use Table 5.1 to analyse the net costs of EU membership subscriptions.

There is some dispute about whether, in today's world of floating exchange rates, the balance of payments is all that significant as an objective of macroeconomic policy. One of the major problems is the unreliability of balance of payments data — statistical corrections are often greater than the values of the individual balances. Perhaps the most useful aspect of the balance of payments is to give an early warning about excess demand (as this tends to show up quickly as a trade deficit), and hence likely inflationary pressure.

There is, however, little doubt that the exchange rate is one of the most significant economic indicators. The exchange rate can appreciate or depreciate rapidly, while domestic prices (particularly wages) are much slower to adjust to shocks. This can cause important imbalances in the economy.

International competitiveness

The performance of the UK on the current account of its balance of payments is crucially affected by its level of international competitiveness. The UK is likely to experience a trade deficit if its exports cannot compete on price in world markets and if imports are challenged only by expensive domestically produced substitutes. The decline in the UK current account in recent years has prompted renewed debate about the failings of UK competitiveness and possible policy remedies.

The real exchange rate

Perhaps the most important overall indicator of UK international competitiveness is the real exchange rate.

- The **real exchange rate** is defined as the nominal exchange rate multiplied by the ratio of UK prices to foreign prices. The nominal exchange rate, which is usually referred to as 'the exchange rate', is simply the number of units of foreign currency that can be obtained for a pound.
- The real exchange rate appreciates if the nominal exchange rate rises or if the UK price level rises relative to the foreign price level. So a rise in the real exchange rate represents a *fall* in international competitiveness.
- A major explanation of the UK's growing trade deficit is the rise in the real exchange rate since 1997, mainly through the rise in the nominal rate — perhaps influenced by the stricter monetary regime imposed by the Labour government.
- A key factor in determining UK competitiveness is **labour productivity**, that is, output per worker. High levels of labour productivity reduce a firm's average costs and so reduce relative export prices and thus the real exchange rate.
- However, high labour productivity is not a sufficient condition for competitiveness. Any productivity advantage will be lost if it is offset by higher wage payments than those received by comparable workers abroad. This aspect of competitiveness is captured by **relative unit labour cost** data.

Other measures of competitiveness

A number of indicators of UK competitiveness are published by the government, all of which have some bearing on the key issues of productivity and relative unit labour costs. The most significant are as follows:

- The degree of **macroeconomic stability**. This is important for encouraging high levels of capital investment, which is, in turn, a determinant of labour productivity.
- The level of **human capital**. The skills and know-how of workers raise their output per hour.
- The level of **capital investment**. A longstanding criticism of the UK economy is that its plants and machinery are out of date compared to those used by its European competitors.
- The **flexibility of the labour market**. A lack of competition in the labour market tends to raise wage rates. UK unemployment rates are currently below those in the rest of the EU, although above those in the USA and Japan.

An appraisal of UK international competitiveness

The UK has achieved greater macroeconomic stability than most of its trading partners in recent years, but remains weak in some microeconomic aspects. The consequence of this has been a rising gap between imports and exports, as shown in the graph below.

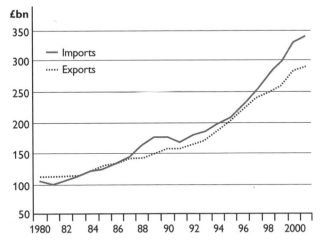

Source: **www.statistics.gov.uk**

UK exports and imports, 1995 prices

The graph shows that although exports have increased steadily in real terms, in recent years imports have grown much more quickly, leading to record trade deficits. In some industries there has been a rapid rise in **import penetration** — a rising ratio of imports to domestic production of the good or service.

Government policy to improve competitiveness

- A low inflation target for monetary policy, to create stability as well as low cost pressures. The Monetary Policy Committee did not feel the need to change interest rates at all in 2002. This is likely to promote investment and thus raise productivity.
- Improving the business environment by encouraging competition and a flexible labour market. The UK loses fewer than 50 working days due to industrial stoppages per 1,000 employees, compared to an EU average of nearly 100.
- Reducing the amount of red tape and the level of taxation on businesses. The increases in employer national insurance contributions in the 2003 Budget will add to business costs.
- Promoting the 'knowledge-driven economy'. This includes the promotion of lifelong learning as workers move between jobs later in life, and encouraging the use of skills such as ICT.
- Tax incentives for firms to increase their expenditure on research and development.
- All successful supply-side policies should — in the long term at least — improve the UK's international competitiveness. However, some of these are very much long term, such as reforms to the education system.
- An emphasis on the quality of products, not just their prices.

Examination skills and concepts

- Understanding the difference between the nominal and the real exchange rate.
- Being able to evaluate alternative measures of international competitiveness.
- Examining the relative importance of productivity and the nominal exchange rate in determining UK competitiveness.
- Being able to assess the role of the UK government in promoting the UK's relative position in international trade.

Common examination errors

- Defining the real exchange rate as simply 'the exchange rate adjusted for inflation'. It is *relative* inflation between the UK and its trading partners that affects competitiveness.
- Confusing the term *productivity* with *production*.
- Thinking that a weak trade performance must be due to declining levels of price competitiveness. A major reason for the increasing UK trade deficit in 2001 and 2002 was the recession in Europe — as EU incomes stagnate, so too do EU countries' demand for UK exports, whether or not they are price competitive.

Useful exercises

- Visit the Department of Trade and Industry (DTI) website on competitiveness at **http://217.154.27.195/competitiveness** and also do a keyword search at **www.dti.gov.uk**. Evaluate the importance of the various measures of competitiveness described by the DTI.
- Assess the extent to which a macroeconomic policy of forcing a depreciation in sterling is likely to improve the UK's long-term international competitiveness. Consider the role of elasticities, the reaction of the UK's trading partners and the likely long-term effect on the real exchange rate.

The UK's international competitiveness is the subject of a great deal of academic research. This topic allows you to make use of both micro- and macroeconomic themes. Not only are there obvious links with topics such as the balance of payments, but the issue of competitiveness also dominates discussion about macroeconomic policy more generally and the question of the UK's membership of the euro in particular.

European monetary union

One of the most interesting economic debates of recent years has been the question of the UK's membership of the euro. The debate goes well beyond economics, into the areas of politics and the issue of national sovereignty.

Advantages of joining the euro

A number of advantages have been suggested were the UK to join the euro:

- Firms relying on exports will no longer have to face **exchange rate instability**. This should promote investment and hence, in the longer term, international competitiveness. In the first year of the euro, sterling was strong and the euro weak. Nonetheless, there is a general feeling that the euro should prove to be more stable than any of the individual currencies it absorbs, due to economies of scale.
- There will be a reduction in **transaction costs**. A single currency eliminates the need to pay commission charges to currency dealers as goods cross borders. This should create a more efficient single market. However, the European Commission estimates that the gain is small, at no more than 0.4% of GDP.
- Increased intra-EU **competition**. The single currency should make price discrimination difficult by making price differences much more obvious to consumers. On the other hand, many other factors will allow the continuation of monopolistic practices: for example, right-hand-drive vs left-hand-drive in the car market.
- Increased **inward direct investment**. Multinational companies may look to euro-zone countries when making future investments.
- Lower **interest rates**. With a credible inflation policy the European Central Bank (ECB) should be able to reduce interest rates. However, the UK's Monetary Policy Committee is generally thought to have outperformed the ECB in the first 2 years of the euro's existence.

Disadvantages of joining the euro

Critics of UK membership of the euro have suggested the following disadvantages:

- The **Stability and Growth Pact** reduces the ability of governments to offset shocks to the economy by counter-cyclical changes in fiscal policy. Under the pact, compulsory for all members of the euro, the government would not be allowed to run a fiscal deficit of more than 3% of GDP. This 'fixed rule' fiscal policy is much more rigid than Gordon Brown's 'golden rule', which allows the government to run up a counter-cyclical deficit. In 2002 Romano Prodi, the European Commission's president, described the Stability Pact as 'stupid'.

- The **recession** experienced by the German economy since 2000 has been blamed partly on the euro. However, the recession may be due to the lagged effects of reunification rather than to euro membership.
- The Monetary Policy Committee has performed well in achieving its inflation target. Critics of the euro compare the ECB's record unfavourably with that of the MPC. The ECB's target is to keep inflation below 2% — there is no targeting band. This may exert a **deflationary bias** in the conduct of European monetary policy. Growth in the rest of Europe has been lower than in the UK since the introduction of the euro-zone.
- The ECB sets interest rates appropriate for the **average** monetary conditions of euro-zone members. From time to time the UK might find itself in a situation that requires a cut in interest rates just when the ECB is raising them. There is certainly a need for the UK to **converge** to a similar macroeconomic condition to other EU members before joining the euro.
- **Asymmetric policy sensitivity**: households in the UK borrow far more on variable-interest loans to finance house purchases than those in the euro-zone (renting is much more popular in the rest of the EU). When the ECB raises rates to combat inflation, consumers in the UK would take a greater burden of adjustment than consumers in the rest of the EU.

There are a number of arguments wrapped up in the euro debate, beyond the purely economic. These include important issues of nationhood, sovereignty and the issue of a federal Europe. These can be indexed in any discussion of the euro, but they should not form the main focus of your analysis in the Unit 6 exam — keep to the economics.

The chancellor's five tests of membership

Gordon Brown has indicated that the following five tests must be satisfied before the UK is likely to benefit from joining the euro and before the government will hold a referendum on the issue:

- Is there **sustainable convergence** between the UK and the euro economies? This test asks whether the UK business cycle is in line with the rest of the EU area, so that interest rates set by the ECB will be suitable for the UK. Under the guidance of the Monetary Policy Committee, UK inflation and growth have been much more stable in recent years — more in line with euro-zone rates.
- Is there **sufficient flexibility** in the UK economy to deal with an asymmetric exogenous shock? That is, can a combination of fiscal policy and market flexibility deal with shocks that hit the UK harder than the other EU economies? The recent deterioration in the UK fiscal position has threatened the UK's ability to pass this test, given the constraints of the Stability and Growth Pact. However, there is some evidence that UK labour markets are more flexible than those in the rest of the EU.

- Will membership of the euro make the UK a more attractive target for **long-term investment**? There seems to be little doubt that membership of the euro is a considerable incentive for multinational investment. Although foreign domestic investment into the UK has been rising in recent years, it has been rising more quickly in Germany.
- Will the **financial services industry** be adversely affected by UK membership of the euro? The City is a major exporter on the UK current account and joining the euro will almost certainly improve its performance. If the UK remains outside the euro, Frankfurt is likely to exploit economies of scale in the provision of financial services.
- The **over-arching test**: will membership of the euro promote UK growth, stability and a lasting increase in jobs? This is really a combination of the previous four tests.

One of the problems of these tests is that they are rather loosely specified both in terms of macroeconomic measurement and in terms of time scale. However, there is general agreement that the UK economy was in a condition that would pass the five tests by 2002. A further issue is the rate at which the UK should join the euro. Joining at too high a rate would lock the economy into an uncompetitive position.

In June 2002 the chancellor added further tests for membership. He said that the Treasury would now also consider the impact of the rapid rise in UK house prices, the significance of the exchange rate, and whether other EU countries were abiding by the terms of the Stability Pact.

Examination skills and concepts
- Evaluating the case for and against UK membership of the euro; being able to examine the relative significance of each of the factors discussed.
- Being able to discuss the controversies surrounding the Stability and Growth Pact. To what extent is observance of the pact by EU members a necessary condition for successful UK membership of the euro-zone?
- Being able to assess the chancellor's five economic tests for euro membership.

Common examination errors
- Treating membership of the euro as a black-and-white issue. There are good arguments on both sides.
- Failing to evaluate the arguments for and against the euro, rather than just listing them.

Useful exercises
- The Council of the European Union's site at **http://ue.eu.int/emu/en/index.htm** contains first-rate background information on the adoption of the euro. Visit the site and collect any evidence that seems to you to help decide the argument.
- Do a search at **www.altavista.co.uk** on the chancellor's five tests for euro entry. Use the suggested links to answer the following: to what extent do the five tests put forward by Gordon Brown adequately capture the issues involved in joining the euro?

This section is concerned with the future role of the UK in the international economy. Will staying outside the euro-zone damage UK growth prospects and even threaten the viability of the UK's long-term membership of the EU? Or will retaining monetary independence give the UK economy greater opportunity for stability and growth?

International trade

International trade is extremely important to the UK economy. On a theoretical level, trade allows greater specialisation and economies of scale from larger markets. The UK's membership of the EU gives it a wide trading zone free of protectionism. In 2001, 49% of UK current account transactions were with other member countries of the EU. However, the EU is a customs union: it imposes tariffs on imports from the rest of the world. This is a potential source of conflict with other trading blocs or large countries, such as the USA, which is the UK's second largest trading partner and accounts for 24% of total balance of payments credits.

The importance of international trade to the UK economy

The traditional theory of international trade centres on the role of comparative advantage in determining the potential gains from trade. The diagram below shows the effect of specialisation and trade for two trading areas, the EU and the USA.

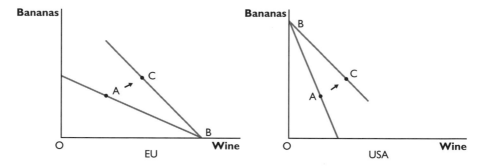

The benefits of specialisation and trade

Suppose that neither area trades and that both are producing at point A on their respective production possibility frontiers (PPFs). Europe has a comparative advantage in producing wine (shown by the shallow gradient of the PPF) and the USA in bananas. If both countries specialise at B on their respective PPFs, they will have an incentive to trade at an exchange rate somewhere in between their respective opportunity cost ratios: for example, along the line from B to C — the same gradient in both diagrams. The result is that *both* trading areas can consume a greater quantity of both bananas and wine.

Trade therefore allows a country to consume beyond its PPF. The greater the gradient of its trading line (BC), the greater the gains from trade to the country concerned. The gradient is measured by the **terms of trade**: an index of export prices divided by an index of import prices. The higher the terms of trade, the greater the quantity of imports a country will be able to acquire for a given volume of exports.

Another way of representing the significance of trade is to show the welfare gain of going from no trade to free trade. The diagram below shows the market for bananas in the EU with no external trade allowed. D_H and S_H represent the domestic demand and supply curves respectively. The price will initially be at P_1 and equilibrium quantity at Q_1. Suppose that trade becomes possible and bananas can be imported at the world price P_W. There will be a gain in consumer surplus of areas $A + B + C$ and a loss of producer surplus of A, implying a net welfare gain of area $B + C$.

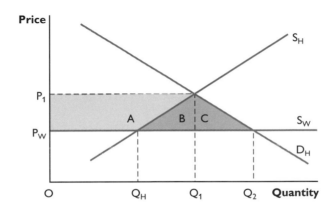

The welfare gain from trade

Trade liberalisation and protectionism

There are many ways in which a country may seek to gain an advantage in world trade by reducing imports:
- **Tariffs** are taxes on imports.
- **Quotas** are quantity restrictions on imports.
- **Export subsidies** are given to firms to give them a competitive advantage when they export to foreign markets.
- **Regulations** — for example, specifying safety rules for the design of goods — can make it very difficult and expensive for foreign firms.

The welfare effect of a tariff

The standard theory of international trade suggests that a tariff reduces welfare. Suppose that the country in the diagram overleaf was initially enjoying free trade. Domestic output would be at Q_H, total demand at Q_1. The distance Q_1–Q_H is the quantity of imports. If the country now puts on a tariff per unit imported equal to the distance P_T–P_W, the domestic price of the good will rise to P_T. This reduces consumer surplus by the area A + B + C + D. However, there is a gain in producer surplus of A as domestic producers expand production to Q_S. The quantity of imports falls to Q_2–Q_S, giving the government the tax revenue C to redistribute to welfare-enhancing causes. The net loss to society is therefore areas B + D.

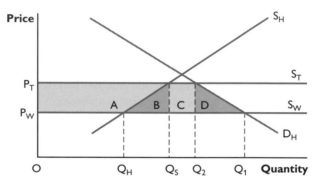

The welfare effect of a tariff

However, a number of issues need to be raised when evaluating the welfare loss from a tariff argument:

- The argument is very static. It suggests that countries should specialise according to their *current* comparative advantages. This may doom some countries to a fixed stage of development.
- The small country assumption can be misleading. The diagram shows a perfectly elastic supply curve from the rest of the world. In a large country, an increase in demand for imports will raise the world price.
- There will be gainers and losers from the abolition of tariffs. The analysis makes the assumption that displaced workers will quickly find jobs in other areas.
- The analysis does not capture all elements of trade: for example, within Europe there are exports of Peugeots from France *and* of BMWs from Germany. There are exports of wine from France to the USA and from the USA to France. It is unlikely that this intra-industry trade is due to differences in opportunity costs.
- Free trade tends to be corrosive of social norms, disturbing traditional cultural practices. There have been many worldwide protests about this in recent years.

The World Trade Organisation (WTO)

At the end of the Second World War, new agreements and institutions were created to try to produce international stability and free trade. One of these agreements was the General Agreement on Tariffs and Trade (GATT), which was designed to encourage a reduction in protectionism. In 1995 the World Trade Organisation was established to act as the convenor of GATT conferences.

- The WTO organises rolling conferences, known as **rounds**, to tackle particular forms of protectionism. These rounds are attended by representatives of the 144 countries currently belonging to the WTO.

- Negotiations are **multilateral**, i.e. they are conducted between many countries rather than just 'bilaterally' between two countries.
- The rounds are conducted on the **most favoured nation** principle. In theory, the offer of a reduction in quotas or tariffs to one country has to be made to all other member countries.
- The current WTO negotiations are known as the **Doha round**. The Doha Development Agenda is being negotiated. Key areas include reductions in agricultural protectionism, the proposed elimination of tariffs on manufactured goods, raising the share of world trade accounted for by services and greater flexibility in intellectual property rights. The original aim of the round was to focus on the problems faced by developing countries and encourage them to reduce agricultural tariffs. However, both the USA and the EU have recently announced further large subsidies for agriculture, making trade agreements in this area much more difficult.

Evaluating the role of the WTO

There are many evaluative points to make about the impact of the WTO on world trade:

- The WTO is particularly important at times of recession in the world economy. It is very tempting for countries to try to isolate themselves from falling demand by increasing protectionism. As countries retaliate, this reduces world trade and inflicts further real damage on the global economy.
- Since the Second World War there have certainly been dramatic reductions in tariffs. The contribution of the WTO to this is, however, probably rather indirect. Countries have tended to reduce protectionism where it was clearly in their interests to do so. The essential problem facing the WTO is that it convenes conferences of **sovereign states**, which tend to act in their own, rather than in general, interests.
- WTO rules allow *regional* reductions in protectionism if this is likely to result in 'substantial' (rather a loose term) areas of free trade. The original intention of GATT was therefore lost as countries took advantage of these rules to form customs unions, such as the EU, and free trade areas, such as NAFTA.
- Some poor countries were allowed to join the WTO with their existing levels of protectionism in place. For example, India still has very high tariffs despite having been one of the first members of the organisation. However, the membership of China was blocked until December 2001 and Russia is still not a member.
- The rules also allowed **special exemptions**: for example, member states are permitted to impose tariffs at times of economic emergency. The USA therefore claims that its recent imposition of steel tariffs is within WTO rules.
- There has also been a worrying rise in non-tariff barriers in recent decades, as countries put in place substitutes for the tariff reductions they have agreed at the WTO. The WTO seems to find it much more difficult to achieve reductions in export subsidies and import regulations than in tariffs. For example, the EU's system of farm subsidies has not been challenged effectively by the WTO and this is the cause of ongoing complaints from the USA. Other countries, such as Japan, have been accused of a 'zero-sum' mentality in trade negotiations, tending to block reform.

These criticisms are made by analysts with a free-trade, neo-liberal point of view. At the same time, in recent years there have been many protests about the activities of the WTO by those who view the process of globalisation in a less positive light.

An important area to consider when evaluating the role of GATT is the relationship between the USA and the EU. This has been the origin of many disputes in the area of international trade in recent years. A good example of this was the controversy over bananas in 1999:

- Bananas produced by US companies (not only in the USA, but also in Latin America) are considerably cheaper than those produced in the Caribbean.
- The EU penalised these bananas with specific tariffs and quotas, favouring instead the produce of former colonies, perhaps as a way of fostering their economic development.
- The WTO ruled against the EU, but the EU was very slow to adjust its policy. The USA retaliated with trade sanctions on specific products from the EU, such as handbags and batteries.
- The role of US fruit-producing companies in Latin America has been extremely controversial. It has been alleged that they often disregard human rights and support unrepresentative regimes.

The impact of trading blocs on the global economy

The growth of free trade areas and customs unions has fundamentally changed the international economy in recent decades:

- Customs unions such as the EU impose a **common external tariff** against imports from outside the bloc. They also tend to give what are in effect export subsidies to their firms; for example, the high level of agricultural subsidies paid as part of the common agricultural policy (CAP). This may encourage trade *within* the bloc, but it distorts trade between the bloc and the rest of the world. Comparative advantages cease to be the basis for trade, and welfare may be reduced.
- Some of the trading blocs are very large, so they benefit from economies of scale. Free trade within these regions may approximate to the benefits of free world trade. However, such arrangements may tend to exclude developing countries.
- The use of protectionism by trading blocs causes **economic inefficiency**, as prices are driven above marginal costs. However, this may be offset to some extent by lower *average* costs due to economies of scale.
- The increased stability from large single-currency zones may bring benefits to participating countries. However, the zones may also discourage competition.

Examination skills and concepts

- Being able to explain the significance of comparative advantage as a basis for analysing the gains from trade.
- Explaining why a country may suffer a welfare loss from the introduction of a tariff, while being able to examine the significance of the assumptions behind this argument.
- Understanding and evaluating the WTO's role in attempting to reduce protectionism.

Common examination errors

- Being unclear that it is comparative rather than absolute advantage that explains the basis of international trade.
- Failing to understand the multilateral nature of WTO trade negotiations.

Useful exercises

- Download and read a chapter from the Oxfam report at **www.maketradefair.com**. Write a review of the 'executive summary'.
- Visit the WTO website at **www.wto.org**. How does this compare with the Oxfam site above?
- Why are intellectual property rights thought to be an increasingly important issue in international trade?
- Use the internet to collect information on the Doha round of the WTO. Start with the WTO site itself. What are the objectives of the round? What has been achieved to date?
- Collect some newspaper articles about any current or recent trade dispute and, for a term, track the consequences for international trade.
- Adapt the diagram showing the welfare effect of a tariff (p. 46) to analyse the welfare effect of a quota.

Linkages and common themes

The issue of international trade is very much part of the topic of globalisation discussed below. You have an opportunity in this area to use the material from Unit 1 on comparative advantage and opportunity costs. There is also a strong link with Unit 5B, Development Economics — the trading relations between the developed and developing worlds are of crucial importance to the world economy.

Globalisation

The term **globalisation** refers to the growing interdependence of countries and the rapid rate of change this brings about. However, globalisation has a number of economic and social aspects, making the term itself rather loose. Key *economic* aspects of globalisation are as follows:

- the growing international division of labour, as countries specialise according to the law of comparative advantage and in search of economies of scale
- the growth of trading blocs such as customs unions and free trade areas, together with the emergence of the large single currency areas such as the euro-zone
- the development of international transport, allowing greater movement of goods and people — both consumers and workers — around the world
- improvements in information technology, allowing rapid communication between all points of the globe
- the increasingly important role of multinational companies

The issues raised by these processes are by no means new. Adam Smith, in *The Wealth of Nations* (1776), described how wealth depends on the extent of the market. There is no point in using efficiency gains from the division of labour unless there are customers to buy the much greater levels of output that this makes possible. This search for customers drives firms from national to international markets and has allowed firms to grow to multinational size with global scales of operation. Such firms often have a market value many times the GDP of some of the countries in which they operate.

Karl Marx, in the *Communist Manifesto* (1848), described the economic and social effects of globalisation. It is well worth considering his analysis that 'all that is solid melts into air' under the forces of global capitalism. Marx also began the study of how globalisation involves **differentiation** of people and countries, as well as rapid change and the sweeping away of traditions. The *Communist Manifesto* is still very interesting reading — the full text is at **www.swan.ac.uk/poli/texts/marx/manic.htm**.

The growing economic interdependence of countries

Participation in global capitalism ties the macroeconomic performance of countries together closely, at least in terms of the regional affiliations. The key features of this economic interdependence are as follows:

- **Very rapid capital mobility.** Speculative 'hot money' flows extremely quickly between countries. This reduces the autonomy of national fiscal and monetary policy. For example, a country maintaining higher interest rates than its major competitors is likely to see an appreciation of its exchange rate and a reduction in its international competitiveness.
- **Multinational investment.** Investors are quick to move funds 'where the action is', becoming intolerant of less well-performing countries. Countries, if only within their trading bloc, now have to compete to attract foreign direct investment from multinationals. This puts pressure on them to conform to certain standards of macroeconomic stability and even political organisation.
- **The growth of world trade and reductions in protectionism.** Much of this has been bilateral, but the role of the WTO may also have been important.

It is argued by many that globalisation is not a new feature of the world economy but one that has continued to evolve from the nineteenth century. Nonetheless, the impact of computerisation does seem to have accelerated some of the processes involved.

The role of MNCs in globalisation

Key characteristics of the role of multinational corporations (MNCs) include the following:

- **Networking between companies.** The complexities of running a global business have resulted in growing networks of partnerships with 'satellite' companies. The 'hubs' of these networks tend to be centred in the USA, the EU and Japan.

- **Decentring of production.** Many multinationals now produce very close to the final market both to cut transport costs and to remain responsive to changes in local tastes. MNCs tend to make regional rather than global decisions about production and consumption.
- **Concentration.** The top 500 multinationals are responsible for 90% of the world's foreign direct investment. The most obvious explanation of this concentration is the economies of scale available to companies operating on a global scale.
- **The 'wild geese' model.** MNCs tend to be footloose, their location being influenced by government subsidies. When these subsidies run out, the companies tend to move on to the next country in the region.

The impact of multinationals on developed economies

MNCs have considerable impact on developed countries, in the following main areas:
- Increases in **investment**. These may be particularly significant for previously underdeveloped areas of the country. There are also likely to be regional multiplier effects, amplifying the benefits to the economy.
- Improvement to the **public finances**. As the level of employment increases, tax revenues will increase from both direct and indirect sources. However, the extent of this improvement depends on the extent of the multinational investment.
- Creating an incentive for countries to make **supply-side improvements**. A country is unlikely to attract foreign direct investment (FDI) if costs of production are higher than in equivalently placed countries. Important costs include wage claims, the burden of government red tape and the expenditure required to overcome planning permission hurdles.
- A positive impact on the **capital account** of the balance of payments, at least in the short run. However, when profits are repatriated this reduces the income surplus on the **current account**.
- The MNC may bring with it world-class **management techniques and technology**. This may have positive spillover effects on indigenous firms. However, in some circumstances the multinational may simply replace local firms.
- A risk of **instability**. In the 1990s, the UK attracted high levels of FDI, with an average of over 25% of all EU multinational investment. However, there were sharp falls in FDI into the UK from American multinationals following the events of 11 September 2001, and these were made worse by the global economic recession and a perception that relative costs in the UK were rising. Some placed additional blame for these falls on the UK's hesitancy about joining the euro.

Evaluating the role of MNCs

The role of MNCs in the global economy is very much a contested issue. Some see the FDI of multinationals as the central pillar of world growth. They cite the role of MNCs in European reconstruction after the Second World War, and also in the Far East in promoting growth during the 1980s. They see multinationals as offering better working conditions and higher rates of pay to local workers.

Critics of MNCs, however, see them as instruments of neo-colonialism, appropriating rent from poor countries and their workers, and repatriating profits to the rich developed countries. A key issue is then the extent to which there is competition *between* MNCs at a regional level. Multinationals have also been accused of homogenising world culture, promoting a rootless and value-free consumer culture, and threatening traditional ways of life.

Examination skills and concepts

- Being able to examine the significance of multinational investment to the UK economy.
- Being in a position to assess the idea that globalisation is a new phenomenon in the world economy.

Common examination errors

- Confusing inward direct investment with official investment (aid).
- Not linking the ideas of international trade and competitiveness to the idea of globalisation.
- Failing to be sufficiently critical of the looseness of the term 'globalisation'.

Useful exercises

- Build up a selection of newspaper articles on selected issues related to globalisation: for example, trade wars between the EU and the USA, the relationship between the West and developing countries, and the issues surrounding the globalisation protests.
- Contrast two modern points of view on globalisation and trace their origins back to Karl Marx and Adam Smith.

Linkages and common themes

The topic of globalisation permits a truly synoptic approach. Do not be afraid to use all of the concepts from other units in your answers to Unit 6.

Questions
&
Answers

This section includes three essay questions and three data-response questions for you to use in your exam preparation. You can use them to check and reinforce understanding of the specification subject matter and to get used to answering questions under timed conditions. You are strongly advised to consult the answers only after you have made your own written responses.

In the examination, you should remember to draw diagrams wherever possible to support your written explanation. This is true for both the essays and the data-response questions. It is worth noting that all the essay sections require evaluative rather than just descriptive answers. Be sure to bring each section to a well-argued conclusion. The data-response questions are similar in style to the questions you can expect in the examination. At the time of writing, all past questions and exemplar papers have had text-only questions.

This section also includes:
- Mark guides and advice on answering essay and data-response questions.
- Sample student answers for each essay and data-response question.
- Examiner's comments on each essay and data-response answer, explaining, where relevant, how the answer could be improved and a higher grade achieved. These comments are preceded by the icon *e*.

Essay questions
Mark guide

There is 1 hour and 45 minutes available for Unit 6. In order to leave time to plan and then check through your answers, you should not write for more than 45 minutes on either section. It is absolutely vital that you split your time between the two sections. Over-running in the essay section could seriously damage your chances of gaining a high grade.

Although the essay you write will be marked out of 100, your total will then be halved. The essay is therefore worth the same as the data-response question, i.e. 50 marks.

There are three essay questions to choose from. Each of these is usually made up of two sub-questions, offering 40 and 60 marks respectively. Both parts are likely to be evaluative, requiring you to prioritise your arguments and come to a conclusion.

Essay-writing tips

- **Allocate your time sensibly** between the two sub-questions of the essay. Spend no more than 20 minutes on a 40-mark question and 30 minutes on a 60-mark question, *including planning*.
- **Plan** the outline of both parts of your answer before you start writing. It is important not to repeat material in the two sections. If you are tempted to do this, you have almost certainly misunderstood the question. Jot down the key paragraph headings of your argument with a few evaluative issues, such as 'elasticities'. Do not write out your plan in longhand — you will not have time. In your plan, remind yourself that you need to write a conclusion.
- Do not be intimidated by the essay mark base of 100. The examiner knows that you have little more than 45 minutes to write the entire essay. You are not expected to write at enormous length: **quality** is much more important than quantity.
- Where appropriate, **draw diagrams** to support your explanation. Some of the theoretical ideas included in the Unit 6 specification are quite difficult. Certainly, they can be difficult to express under timed conditions in an examination. Diagrams carry a lot of the explanation for you. Use them, and include arrows marking the changes that have taken place. Key diagrams in this unit include the AD/AS model and the welfare effect of a tariff, but because the unit is synoptic you should use *any* economics diagram that is relevant: for example, supply and demand or negative externalities. Make sure that each diagram has the axes labelled properly.
- Leave plenty of space for each diagram you use and give it an explanatory title. Double-check that you have labelled the axes correctly.

- Always **define the key economic terms** you have encountered in the question. There are often marks reserved for this in the examiner's mark scheme. Failure to define key terms is one of the most common reasons for otherwise very strong candidates dropping marks.
- Remember that 30% of the marks in Unit 6 are for **evaluation**. Prioritise your arguments and assess the relative strengths and weaknesses of each factor you discuss.
- Write legibly and avoid using handwriting that is too small. It is surprising how difficult some candidates make it for the examiner to read their scripts.

Essay structure

It is important to impose a convincing structure on your essay's line of argument:

- Begin each sub-question with a brief introduction. This should define any key terms in the question and state the central themes of the essay.
- Divide each part of your essay into three or four key paragraphs in which you introduce different facets of your argument.
- Include evaluation material in *each* of these paragraphs. Do not leave all your evaluation to a separate paragraph.
- Finish your answer to each sub-question with a formal conclusion. This is the time to come off the fence, to leave behind discussion of the pros and cons of your argument and decide where you stand. Which of the arguments you have presented is most convincing?

Question 1

UK international competitiveness

(a) Evaluate **two** alternative measures of the competitive position of the leading
   countries in international trade. (40 marks)
(b) To what extent is the exchange rate the key factor in determining the
   competitiveness of British industry in overseas markets? (60 marks)

■ ■ ■

Candidate's answer

(a) The success of a country in international trade comes down to two key factors,
price and quality. However, these are not absolute issues: what matters is a
country's performance *relative* to its trading partners. In this essay two measures
of price competitiveness will be discussed, the real exchange rate and relative
normalised unit labour costs.

> **e** This is an ideal introduction, short but to the point. The key issue — relative prices
> — is identified and two measures are signposted. The examiner will be able to
> follow this candidate's response with little difficulty.

The real exchange rate measures the nominal exchange rate adjusted by relative
price levels:

$$\text{real exchange rate} = \text{nominal exchange rate} \times \frac{\text{UK price level}}{\text{foreign price level}}$$

If the real exchange rate appreciates then the level of international competitiveness falls. For example, if the UK and foreign price levels are rising at the same
rate then a higher exchange rate will make UK exports more expensive relative
to goods produced by our competitors. Alternatively, if the nominal exchange rate
is unchanged, UK inflation rising above the inflation rate of our trading partner
will also reduce our competitiveness by raising the relative price of our exports
and making foreign goods cheaper relative to domestically produced goods. The
real exchange rate is usually expressed as an index number to show percentage
changes.

However, the real exchange rate is a very high-level measure of competitiveness.
On the one hand, it captures a key aspect of whether the UK will be able to compete
in international trade. On the other hand, data showing a rise in the real exchange
rate do not explain the background causes of the appreciation. Further, it is often
the case that, particularly in the short run, changes in the nominal exchange rate
are driven by speculators rather than by underlying competitiveness. Short-run

changes in the real exchange rate may therefore carry little information about long-run changes. It is also the case that not all goods are traded — the ratio in the definition should, perhaps, be the price level of traded goods rather than all goods.

This is an excellent beginning. The definition is expressed clearly and explained properly. The two elements of the measure are described and applied correctly to the issue of international competitiveness. There could, perhaps, have been some mention of the 'leading countries' part of the question. The candidate has included a convincing paragraph evaluating the measure from a number of points of view, showing a sophisticated understanding of the limitations of these kinds of aggregate measure.

A second measure of international competitiveness is relative normalised unit labour costs (RNULC). This measures labour costs per unit of output in the UK relative to those in our trading partners. To standardise the two costs that will first be measured in different currencies, the figures have to be 'normalised', i.e. expressed in a single currency.

However, there are a few problems with this measure. First, are the data from the two countries being compared collected on the same basis? Second, which exchange rate should be used to make the comparison — the current exchange rate or the purchasing power parity rate? Third, labour costs are only one aspect of competitiveness — a general problem once one moves away from the real exchange rate measure. Fourth, there is no automatic relationship between the costs of producing exports and their *prices* — there can be variations in profit mark-ups between countries.

This is another first-rate paragraph. Once again, the definition is expressed clearly and there is a sustained attempt at evaluation. The issues raised apply to most measures of international competitiveness.

Score for part (a): 38/40 marks = strong grade A

(b) There are a number of factors determining the competitiveness of the UK in overseas markets, of which the exchange rate is an important but not the most crucial factor. The UK can have a very high exchange rate but still be competitive in international markets if it has low costs of production and a high quality of product. Indeed, a high exchange rate can be an indicator of competitiveness rather than a threat to it.

This is a good introduction that contains a key evaluative point — that an appreciation of the exchange rate can be a consequence of improved competitiveness rather than a cause of loss of competitiveness. There is some indication of where the rest of the essay is headed, but this is not so clearly signposted as in the introduction to the previous answer.

The exchange rate is the rate at which foreigners have to surrender their currency for pounds. As the value of sterling increases, so too does the cost of acquiring pounds. Other things remaining equal, a rise in the pound will make UK exports less competitive. For example, the UK does approximately half of its trade with other members of the EU. The rise of the value of sterling against the euro in 2000–01, caused by pessimism about the state of the euro-zone economy and confidence in the performance of the Monetary Policy Committee, happened at the same time as a growing trade deficit with Europe. However, this kind of correlation does not necessarily imply a causation. There are a number of other factors that will determine competitiveness.

e This paragraph makes a number of important points, and ends with a suitable piece of evaluation. There is, however, a certain amount of digression towards the end: the question did not ask about the causes of the appreciation of sterling.

The first of these is labour productivity (as measured by RNULC described above). If the output per worker in the UK is low compared to that in the economies of our overseas competitors then exporters will find it more difficult to compete on price. Of course, high levels of labour productivity are not sufficient to ensure competitiveness — the quality of the product and other costs are also very important. Nonetheless, low labour productivity is often seen as the Achilles heel of UK manufacturing. Recent data in *The Economist* showed the UK lagging behind America by up to 40% in this area.

A number of factors cause poor performance in relative labour productivity. Governments used to place much of the blame on the trade unions. Restrictive working practices and industrial stoppages were more common before the reforms to labour law in the 1980s. However, the UK now has better labour relations than many of its trading partners.

e There is a small error here. RNULC measures relative unit labour costs. Labour productivity is only one aspect of this. Wage rates are also important: the two *together* determine RNULC. However, these paragraphs contain an excellent discussion of the importance of labour productivity, with plenty of evaluation and a broad selection of relevant factors. The candidate is likely to achieve extra marks for a relevant current reading from *The Economist* magazine or website.

Of more concern today, perhaps, is the low level of skills of UK workers. The relative amounts of *human capital* are a key determinant of international competitiveness, affecting both the relative price and the relative quality of exports. There has been great emphasis by government on the importance of the 'knowledge-driven economy' in creating a flexible workforce in recent years.

e This is an important point, but there is no explicit evaluation of the role of human capital.

The level of investment in capital machinery is also a major determinant of competitiveness, particularly in the long run. Having up-to-date technology is important both to keep costs down and to be able to make products that can compete on quality. The level of investment is, in turn, affected by the macroeconomic condition of the economy and, in particular, by the level of interest rates set by the Monetary Policy Committee. This shows that macroeconomic conditions can have a key role in determining international competitiveness.

There are a number of other factors that play a role in determining competitiveness. The degree of competition domestically is important because it may discipline firms to cut costs and avoid large mark-ups over costs. The amount of red tape and bureaucracy, e.g. health and safety legislation, imposed on the running of businesses will affect costs. The level of tax incentives for companies to spend profits on research and development will have some effect on the level of innovation of product design.

In conclusion, there are a very large number of factors that contribute to the competitive position of the UK in international markets. Of these, the exchange rate is an important factor but labour productivity has even more significance. It is possible to argue that a high exchange rate encourages competitiveness by forcing firms to cut costs. However, labour productivity is itself influenced by a number of less individually important factors.

🅔 This is an excellent section, covering many of the major points. There is no expectation that all the factors affecting competitiveness could be addressed in the time available, but the candidate picks some important ones and discusses them fully. The answer is distinguished by its high level of evaluation. With the exception of the paragraph on human capital, all the paragraphs discuss the relative significance of the factors chosen. A formal conclusion is presented, prioritising the issues discussed.

Score for part (b): 50/60 marks = grade A

Total scored: 88/100 marks = grade A

Question 2
Macroeconomic imbalance and the threat of deflation

(a) **During 2002 the UK economy experienced strong growth in retail sales, a decline in manufacturing output and a rapidly rising trade deficit. Examine the factors that might have led to these imbalances.** (40 marks)

(b) **To what extent can changes in government policy deal with such imbalances without leading to deflation?** (60 marks)

■ ■ ■

Candidate's answer

(a) The UK economy in 2002 saw consumer spending rise rapidly but output by manufacturing fell. This created a number of imbalances in the economy: the decline in manufacturing was accompanied by strong growth in the service sector. Inflation stayed close to the 2.5% target but service sector prices rose faster than that, whilst the prices of many goods actually fell. Exports grew very slowly and imports accelerated. The main factors behind these imbalances were the housing market and the exchange rate. The decline in manufacturing can also be seen as part of a long-term problem facing the UK.

   🖉 This is a good introduction. Wherever possible the candidate should use knowledge from the UK economy, although the data might have been better used later in the essay. The nature of the imbalances is elaborated and the main factors are identified. There is a hint of the direction that the evaluation might take.

Probably the major cause of the growth in retail sales was the performance of the housing market. House prices in 2002 grew at annual rates as high as 20%. Because the majority of UK households live in owner-occupied dwellings, an increase in house prices represents a substantial increase in wealth.

   Often, people will have seen their house value rise by more than their annual earnings. This boosts retail sales in a number of ways. As wealth rises, people may feel more confident about spending. It was noticeable that measures of consumer confidence remained high in 2002 despite problems in the rest of the economy. Second, a large part of the increase in consumption in 2002 was financed by record increases in consumer credit: people were happy to increase their borrowing given the surge in the value of their principal asset. Third, a number of people took out extra borrowing secured on their property.

   This increase in house prices was offset to some extent by a significant fall in the stock market as the FTSE followed other markets. However, most people's houses are worth far more than their share portfolios so the fall in the stock market did not do more than dent the growth in retail sales. However, the fall in the FTSE may well have limited business investment by making new financing more difficult.

The growth in retail sales was caused by a number of other factors. Employment grew to a record high in 2002 — and unemployment continued to fall. With secure incomes to look forward to, people are more inclined to take out credit. At the same time, nominal interest rates were at a record low of only 4% throughout 2002, making borrowing look very cheap — although with inflation nearer 2% these rates were still positive in real terms.

e This is a good section on the growth in retail sales and it scores high marks for evaluation because the various factors are examined for their relative significance. However, this answer is getting a little long for the time available — it is better to cover a number of factors rather than just one or two.

At the same time, the UK experienced a high level of the exchange rate with £1 continuing to be worth between 1.50 and 1.60 euros, probably rather above purchasing power parity levels. Background causes of the high value of sterling included confidence in the UK economy and high interest rates relative to those in the rest of the EU. The over-valued pound is a major problem for UK manufacturers who rely on exports for a substantial part of their sales, and goes a long way to explain the fall in manufacturing output that occurred in 2002.

The overall picture is therefore one of rising demand for goods and services, but with a tendency for the goods to come from abroad, made cheaper to UK consumers by the high value of sterling. Thus goods prices have been falling and service prices rising.

e This is a good section, but the main point is left until right at the end. There is evaluation throughout. However, there was scope for mentioning more about the policy environment and other factors keeping the exchange rate high. There is also the possibility that goods prices have been falling because of supply-side improvements. The candidate's introduction suggested that there would be some consideration of longer-term processes of deindustrialisation, but these never appeared in the main part of the essay. Nonetheless, in the time available this is a very creditable attempt.

Score for part (a): 31/40 marks = good grade A

(b) A number of policy measures might reduce these imbalances. However, they are likely to involve some degree of cuts in consumer spending. If this takes place too quickly then confidence could be adversely affected in circumstances where households are sitting on a record level of debt. This could then lead to rapid falls in aggregate demand and the risk of deflation. Deflation is where prices fall — and in this case the threat is that real output may also fall.

e This introduction summarises some of the main issues reasonably well and has the virtue of defining deflation. However, there should have been some mention of the policy dilemma faced by the Monetary Policy Committee. If the MPC cuts interest rates to reduce the value of sterling and make exports more competitive, it runs the risk of fuelling the demand for housing. If it raises rates to cool the housing market, this could lead to rapid rises in sterling and an even faster collapse of manufacturing.

The government could use tighter fiscal policy to address the issue. Consumer spending could be reined in by higher levels of income tax. However, there is often little political room for manoeuvre here and the effects might take some time to have their full impact. It is also likely that such a policy would have only a small effect on the exchange rate.

On the monetary side, the MPC could raise interest rates to try to stop the rise in house prices. However, the MPC's objective is the overall level of inflation and this remains below the 2.5% target set by the government. Raising interest rates might well take inflation below 1.5% and even into deflation. The main risk is that the housing market bubble will burst, with many people tempted to sell, believing that house values have peaked. This then has a knock-on effect into consumption: people with large debts will see their wealth fall sharply and may be forced to cut back on consumption quite severely. Many people have borrowed more than their house might be worth in such a collapse, leaving them with negative equity.

🖉 This section contains good material on the potential for the house market boom to go into reverse, but it misses the trade-off between lower house prices and a rising exchange rate. Higher interest rates would be likely to attract 'hot money' flows, boosting the value of sterling and making manufacturing less competitive.

A further policy option would be for the government to use supply-side policies to raise the competitiveness of manufacturers. Policies might include measures to increase market efficiency, incentives and granting subsidies for research and development. The use of supply-side policies, if effective, would reduce the rate of inflation but allow an increase in output as manufacturers become more internationally competitive. However, the full impact of such policies would take a long time to show through.

In conclusion, the government has a dilemma. It has allowed a loosening of fiscal policy by increasing government spending. This has been accompanied by a dramatic rise in house prices and increases in consumer credit. To prevent aggregate demand getting totally out of control in these circumstances, the MPC has had to maintain relatively high levels of interest rates. This has kept sterling high, much to the disadvantage of manufacturing industry. Of the policies discussed, a tightening of fiscal policy and a loosening of monetary policy seems the most appropriate. The supply-side policies would take far too long to implement.

🖉 Overall, this is a slightly uneven answer, which contains many good points but does not make enough of the conflict between objectives indicated by the question. The answer badly needs some aggregate demand and supply diagrams to make some of the points clearer. However, the candidate reaches a reasonable conclusion and shows some evaluation throughout.

Score for part (b): 35/60 marks = grade C

Total scored: 66/100 marks = grade A

Question 3

Globalisation and EU membership

(a) Examine the factors contributing to the process of globalisation. (40 marks)

(b) To what extent does the UK's membership of the EU, whilst at the same time maintaining an independent currency, allow it to benefit fully from the process of globalisation? (60 marks)

■ ■ ■

Candidate's answer

(a) Globalisation is a very broad term — some would say too broad to be all that analytically useful — which refers to the growing interdependence of countries, the growth of trade, the dominance of multinational companies, the emergence of ever-larger trading blocs such as the EU and the mobility of international capital. This process is by no means new, but in some areas it has accelerated in recent years due to improvements in information technology and the cumulative effects of international capitalism.

> **e** This is a good introduction, which tackles the term 'globalisation' and suggests that it has many aspects. It also contains two key elements of evaluation in this area: the idea that globalisation is nothing new and the suspicion that the term is too broad to allow precise analysis. There could, perhaps, have been more attention to the variety of factors at work behind the process.

Ever since Adam Smith wrote *The Wealth of Nations* in 1776, the working model of capitalism has contained an assumption that the scope of the market determines the extent to which firms can profit from the division of labour. The logic of this is that firms will seek *international* markets and grow to a size appropriate for this. The growth of international trade that prompted (and in turn was made possible by) innovations in transport in the nineteenth century grew further in the twentieth century, particularly with the arrival of jet aircraft. In this sense the idea of globalisation is nothing new — it was a process already well understood by Adam Smith and Karl Marx.

The invention first of computers and then of the internet in the second half of the twentieth century accelerated this process even more, allowing multinational firms to coordinate production in highly dispersed parts of the world. Again, the evolution of this technology was probably both the cause and consequence of globalisation.

However, at the same time as the growth in world trade and the emergence of the multinationals, there has been an increase in the importance of trading blocs in the form of either free trade areas or customs unions (which impose a common external tariff on non-members). Many of these are continuing to grow at a considerable pace. For example, the EU has recently agreed that a number of former Iron-Curtain states such as Latvia can join in 2004, Turkey's membership is being discussed, and Russia has expressed an interest. The free trade areas within these blocs offer tremendous economies of scale to firms located inside them. They also tend to become common currency zones, for example the euro-zone, so reducing transaction costs and potentially creating greater macroeconomic stability.

A further factor often put forward for the increase in world trade since the Second World War was the role of the World Trade Organisation (formerly GATT). As part of the process of trade expansion there has certainly been a reduction in tariffs over the past few decades. However, these have often been negotiated bilaterally or as part of a trading bloc. Protectionism *between* trading blocs is still rife, as the recent steel disputes between the USA and EU illustrate, although these are often in the form of production subsidies rather than overt tariffs — especially in the area of agricultural trade.

Of these factors by far the most important is the logic of trade itself. All the rest can be seen as developments to enable greater trade, a larger scale of operation and the need to establish immediate lines of communication between different countries. In my view, technology did not determine this process; the adoption of the technology was part of the process itself.

e This is an excellent answer, covering most of the key points. There could, perhaps, have been a short paragraph on the importance of capital mobility, which has been a factor in promoting the growth of larger currency zones. The answer scores high marks for evaluation throughout.

Score for part (a): 35/40 marks = grade A

(b) The UK is a member of the EU customs union. This gives it many advantages in the area of international trade. On the other hand, the UK has postponed joining the euro because governments believe that the costs would outweigh the benefits. In the long term, the decision to stay outside the euro-zone could damage the possibilities for growth in trade and, more significantly, threaten the UK's position both as a financial centre and as a target for multinational investment.

e This introduction sets out the issues to be discussed in the main part of the essay. There is a clear statement of the dilemma faced by an EU country that remains outside the euro-zone. The prioritisation of arguments ensures that this part of the answer earns evaluation marks.

Membership of the EU gives the UK many of the benefits from the processes of globalisation discussed in the first part of the essay. The EU is a customs union which offers free trade to all member countries. Although there are occasional non-tariff barriers within the EU (e.g. the Anglo-French beef disputes), these tend to be minor relative to the extent of trade as a whole. The UK's membership of the EU allows it to increase specialisation in the direction of comparative advantage and to benefit from economies of scale. This is a very important issue now that the EU is expanding to include many eastern European countries, such as Poland and Czechoslovakia.

It is also a key issue given the rise of other trading blocs such as NAFTA. Joining a trading bloc seems to be a prerequisite of participating in the process of globalisation.

The decision not to join the euro has not threatened these benefits all that much. The most obvious problem of staying outside the euro-zone is the continuing transaction costs this imposes on exporters who have to switch between currencies. However, the EU Commission itself has estimated that such costs only comprise about 0.4% of GDP.

A more significant issue is the potential exchange rate volatility between sterling and the euro. The strength of sterling in the first few years of the euro's existence has certainly limited UK exports. However, although sterling has been high, it has not been particularly unstable — both the UK and the euro-zone have stabilising fixed-rule monetary policies.

> 🖉 This is a good approach to the question, weighing up the two aspects of the UK's membership of the EU and relating them to trade — a key aspect of globalisation. The answer would benefit from greater consideration of the strategic issues of joining/staying outside trading blocs.

A further issue is the loss of price transparency that keeping a separate currency involves. This tends to reduce competition and to increase the likelihood that the UK will be the target of price discrimination. However, information failures of this sort are likely to persist even if the UK were to join the euro: cultural differences such as driving on different sides of the road make this inevitable.

London's position as a financial centre and as a major source of service sector exports has been threatened by the UK's delay in joining the euro. There has been some suggestion that Frankfurt may gain at London's expense in this area. However, 2 years into the euro there is little sign that London's position is being eroded.

Perhaps the most significant long-term issue is whether foreign direct investment (FDI) into the UK by multinationals will be discouraged if we stay outside the euro-zone. This comes down to costs (e.g. wage increases) and stability: if the UK can compete in these areas then there seems little reason for multinationals to go elsewhere in the EU. The more important factor for them is likely to be producing inside the tariff wall rather than the common currency zone. However, a number of recent high-profile decisions by multinationals to leave the UK on the basis of costs (e.g. BMW) are a worrying development.

In conclusion, the benefits to be gained from globalisation in this area are increased trade, greater international competition and multinational investment. All of these are more heavily influenced by the UK's membership of the EU trading bloc than by the question of its membership of the euro. Only if a refusal to participate in the latter threatened our membership of the former would there be any cause for concern.

e This is a strongly argued essay with a very evaluative conclusion. It would strengthen the essay if more examples were included to illustrate the points being made — for example, if the candidate supplied data on multinationals.

Score for part (b): 44/60 marks = grade A

Total scored: 79/100 = grade A

Data-response questions
Mark guide

The data-response section is worth the same as the essay — 50 marks. It is very important that you allocate a full 50 minutes to your answer.

There are two data-response questions to choose from. You will probably not have time to read through the entire text of each before choosing. However, there is time to assess the subject matter of each question and to check that you can have a go at each of the sub-questions. *Always* choose a question where you have something to say in response to all the questions rather than one where you can only do some parts.

Tips for answering data-response questions

- Allocate your time sensibly between the sub-questions. Allow a maximum of 1 minute per mark. Only spend 10 minutes on a section worth 10 marks.
- It is much better to write half a page on each of two sub-questions for 10 marks than a whole page on one sub-question and nothing on the other because of shortage of time. This is because it is much easier to pick up marks at the beginning of an answer than at the end.
- Be sure to obey the instructions in the question. If you are asked to use evidence from the passage or data, then do so explicitly — for text, use quotation marks. If you are asked to draw a diagram, make sure you do not forget to include one in your answer.
- Watch out for changes in keywords as you work through the data-response. It is likely that early sections will ask for no more than knowledge and application. In later sections, however, there will be analysis and evaluation questions. It is essential that you adapt your response to these keywords.
- For analysis questions ('analyse', 'explain' etc.), always try to draw a relevant theory diagram with which to anchor your answer. These really are often worth a thousand words and so greatly reduce the burden of explanation. Remember that this is a synoptic module, so both microeconomic and macroeconomic diagrams may be appropriate.
- For evaluation questions ('assess', 'examine' etc.), remember to look at the pros and cons of the arguments presented and to come to a brief conclusion, prioritising the factors you have discussed.
- You may find it helps to start each data-response section on a new page of the answer booklet. That way you can go back and extend your answers if you have time at the end.

Question 1

UK monetary and fiscal policy

Extract 1: The Monetary Policy Commitee

After many years in which monetary policy was the only game in town, the focus has shifted. Suddenly, fiscal policy is in the spotlight. TrG

The focus on fiscal policy is understandable. Observing monetary policy this year has been like watching a slow-drying paint become safe to touch. The Bank of England, like the Federal Reserve and European Central Bank, has not changed interest rates this year. I grew up on rates changing a couple of times a month.

Sir Edward George now has a distinctly 'steady Eddie' view on interest rates, implying it will take a lot to shift them either way. The stock market's steadier performance in recent days will provide a further argument for holding rates steady. With only two more Monetary Policy Committee meetings this year, we could see a full calendar year without a change in interest rates, which has not happened since 1959.

On the fiscal side, however, things do not seem so predictable. Gordon Brown won plaudits for his tight control of the public finances during the last parliament and has continued to operate with low levels of public debt — 30% of GDP — and a surplus on his budget. Now, however, concern is growing. Figures on Friday showed public sector net borrowing of more than £5bn last month, the highest for 9 years.

A recent report by Ernst and Young suggests that the deficit may rise as high as £7bn for the current fiscal year, and that the situation may well repeat itself in the following year as weak tax revenues combine with strong growth in government spending. The chancellor will be in danger of breaching his 'golden rule' unless he raises taxes in the spring budget.

Source: *The Sunday Times*, 20 October 2002.

Extract 2: The UK house price boom

While Britain's housing boom shows little sign of flagging, the property market's strength is now prompting fears that a slump could tip the country into deflation. As confidence in the strength of the global recovery has ebbed away, fears have grown that the USA and Europe may be in for Japanese-style deflation: a general fall in prices, accompanied by economic stagnation, which is difficult to cure.

'The biggest danger of deflation in the UK is if the housing market topples over, leaving consumers with huge indebtedness,' said John Butler of HSBC. 'It would mean a repeat of the early 1990s, in which consumers would not respond to interest rates, and just would not spend.'

data-response question 1

> If deflation does occur, the real value of debt will rise — making consumers even more likely to cut back on their spending.
>
> Source: *Financial Times*, 21 August 2002.

(a) (i) Distinguish between monetary policy and fiscal policy. (4 marks)

    (ii) Explain the role of the Monetary Policy Committee in the conduct of monetary policy. (6 marks)

(b) Examine the factors that caused the MPC to leave interest rates unchanged during 2002. (10 marks)

(c) Assess reasons why the UK's fiscal position deteriorated in 2002. (10 marks)

(d) Evaluate the use of the 'golden rule' in the conduct of fiscal policy. (10 marks)

(e) Examine the potential for monetary and fiscal measures to deal with deflation. (10 marks)

■ ■ ■

Candidate's answer

(a) (i) Monetary policy is usually conducted via the central bank — in the UK's case, the Bank of England. Monetary instruments include changes in interest rates, attempts to influence the money supply and use of foreign exchange reserves to alter the exchange rate. Fiscal policy is conducted by the government — through the Treasury. Fiscal instruments include changes to the level or composition of taxation and changes in government spending. **4/4 marks**

e This is a good response. It is important not to spend too long on the early sections of data-response questions.

(ii) The Monetary Policy Committee was given independence over the conduct of monetary policy in 1997. Its role is to achieve an inflation target set by the government. The target is currently to achieve 2.5% inflation as measured by the RPIX plus or minus 1%. The only instrument available to the MPC is changes in interest rates. If inflation is rising above 2.5% then interest rates will be raised — so reducing the growth of aggregate demand. If the inflation rate goes outside the target band then the governor of the Bank of England must write an 'open letter' to the chancellor explaining the MPC's failure. **6/6 marks**

e This is another excellent response, succinct but covering the main issues at stake.

(b) Perhaps the most important factor in the MPC's decision to leave interest rates unchanged in 2002 was the fact that inflation was below target for most of the year. This made any increase in interest rates impossible. With inflation below target, real GDP growth at only 1.6% — way below the trend average of 2.4% — and the FTSE-100 suffering a sustained fall, the MPC would have been tempted to cut interest rates. However, the housing market was still showing signs of overheating throughout the year. A cut in interest rates, it was feared, would cause further rapid increases in house values and threaten a much more severe adjustment when the 'bubble' burst. **7/10 marks**

e This answer discusses the two main sets of factors influencing the MPC's decision to leave interest rates unchanged. A brief mention of the growing trade deficit as another signal suggesting the dangers of cutting rates would have added to the answer.

(c) The UK fiscal position deteriorated sharply in 2002 to a forecast £20bn deficit following several years of surplus. There are two key reasons why this happened. The first was the very large increase in government spending on health and education begun in 2002. At the same time, although on a smaller scale, there were increases in other elements of government spending, in particular transport and the police.

The second reason was the world recession that began to dampen UK growth rates and so led to a fall in tax revenues. With incomes growing more slowly, so too did income tax revenues. Meanwhile, consumption remained relatively strong — it was much more a fall in direct than indirect tax revenues that explains the deficit. **5/10 marks**

e This answer is very much along the right lines. However, it lacks some detail. A larger number of factors could have been discussed and rather more data from the UK economy might have been introduced.

(d) The 'golden rule' was made a main plank of fiscal policy by Gordon Brown in 1997. The rule states that government borrowing may not, on average over the business cycle, exceed that required to finance net public sector investment — i.e. spending required to add to the stock of public sector capital in the form of new hospital buildings, roads etc.

The first advantage of such a rule is that it should limit the scope for running up large fiscal deficits (often a feature of politically motivated fiscal policy in the past) and thus ensure a high level of confidence in the running of the UK economy. However, the very large deficit (greater than the passage suggests) announced in late 2002 suggests that the rule may give the chancellor too much room for manoeuvre.

A second advantage is the effect that such a fixed rule should have on confidence in the City and among consumers. If the rule is believed then tax cuts or changes in government spending will not be discounted and so should have a powerful effect. On the other hand, with a rising deficit the credibility of the rule is not 100%. **8/10 marks**

e This is a very good response. The answer begins with a precise definition of the 'golden rule'. It then treats the question in an evaluative way, looking at the pros and cons of such fixed-rule policy regimes. However, there is no discussion of the strength of the rule in allowing automatic stabilisers to work effectively.

ata-response question 1

(e) Deflation occurs when the price level in the economy actually falls, i.e. there is negative inflation. This can be accompanied by falling real GDP if the deflation is caused by falls in aggregate demand, or rising real GDP if the cause is a rise in aggregate supply. The effectiveness of monetary or fiscal policy depends on the kind of deflation the economy is experiencing.

This is a good start, with a discussion of the meaning of 'deflation'.

For deflation caused by rising aggregate supply, all the government has to do is ensure that there is a corresponding rise in aggregate demand to stop falls in the price level as output increases. An appropriate monetary policy would be to cut interest rates to stimulate consumption and investment and, by reducing the value of sterling as hot money moves out of the country, increasing exports and reducing imports. This could also be achieved through a fiscal expansion — higher government spending or lower taxes — although a reduction in interest rates would have the added benefit of raising aggregate supply further in the long term through increased investment.

Dealing with deflation caused by falls in aggregate demand is much more difficult. A reduction in interest rates might well have little effect (as has recently been the case in Japan) because consumer confidence is *already* undermined. Monetary policy in this case is like 'pushing on the end of a piece of string' as Keynes memorably put it. Fiscal policy is likely to be more effective because government can spend to replace the expenditure of pessimistic households. There may be a low multiplier, but at least the initial spending will show up as greater aggregate demand. However, big increases in the fiscal deficit may be difficult in circumstances where falling incomes have already greatly reduced the tax take.

8/10 marks

This is an excellent answer, with a great deal of evaluation. If a couple of diagrams had been included to illustrate the AD/AS analysis, this answer would have been awarded full marks.

Total scored: 38/50 = grade A

Question 2

The Stability and Growth Pact

Extract 1: The German public sector deficit

Less than a month after narrowly securing re-election, Germany's finance minister, Hans Eichel, has dropped two bombshells: tax rises and cuts in spending to cover a 14bn euro gap in next year's budget, and news that Germany will this year fail to hold its deficit within the rules for Europe's common currency.

Both detonations are still resonating around the country and Europe. Domestic voters, promised by Mr Eichel's Social Democratic Party that there would be no tax rises and that this year's fiscal deficit was under control, feel cheated. Outside Germany, those still backing the Stability and Growth Pact are shocked that its architect envisages one of the most flagrant breaches.

It is on the revenue side that Mr Eichel is under the heaviest fire. Faltering growth has led to collapsing tax revenues, which will blow a hole in Germany's commitment to hold its budget deficit within 3% of GDP. Next year also looks bleak. Mr Eichel has abandoned the government's 2.5% growth forecast in favour of 1.5%, triggering massive revisions to his draft 2003 budget. Business and taxpayers' lobbies are up in arms.

The German government insists that it remains committed to the Stability Pact, and Mr Eichel believes that Germany will balance its budget by 2006: 'The economy goes in cycles, as does the finance minister. We are in a period of bad weather. But what's the alternative? To give up? That's not going to happen.'

Source: *Financial Times*, 21 October 2002.

Extract 2: Gordon Brown attempts to redraw euro-zone rules

The chancellor is mounting an attempt to change European Union budget rules. Treasury sources admit he is likely to fail and that failure would serve to delay further Britain's entry into the single European currency.

Gordon Brown will try to convince other EU members to change the Stability and Growth Pact, which stipulates that members of the euro-zone must keep their budget deficits below 3% of GDP, move towards balanced budgets over time, and ensure that the overall level of government debt is kept to 60% of GDP.

The chancellor is highly critical of the Stability Pact because it places constraints on the amount a country can spend on public services without putting up taxes. Brown is committed to additional spending to reform the National Health Service and is

ata-response question 2

worried that the pact would eventually be used against him. He has said that the pact should be more flexible and, like the 'golden rule', should take into account the economic cycle.

Source: *The Business*, 7 October 2002.

(a) (i) **Define the term 'fiscal deficit'.** (4 marks)

(ii) **Explain why reductions in economic growth may cause a deterioration in the fiscal position.** (6 marks)

(b) **Assess the likely impact of faltering growth in the German economy on the UK economy.** (10 marks)

(c) **Assess the importance of the Stability and Growth Pact to the success of the euro-zone.** (10 marks)

(d) **Evaluate the 'golden rule' for fiscal policy adopted by the UK government.** (10 marks)

(e) **To what extent would joining the euro make the control of UK inflation more effective?** (10 marks)

■ ■ ■

Candidate's answer

(a) (i) The economy's fiscal position is the difference between the level of government spending and tax revenue. A deficit refers to a situation where spending exceeds revenue — the difference being made up by borrowing (selling gilts) or, in more extreme cases, printing money. **4/4 marks**

e Full marks are given for a succinct and convincing answer.

(ii) Economic growth is the rate at which real GDP is rising in an economy. A fall in economic growth means that real GDP is rising less quickly. This in turn means that incomes will be rising less quickly and that government tax revenue will grow by less than originally forecast. There may also be a fall in the rate of growth of consumption (although borrowing may make up the gap), so reducing expected revenue from indirect tax. The slowdown is likely to be accompanied by a rising output gap and, eventually, rising unemployment. This will make the deficit worse by raising government expenditure on benefits. **6/6 marks**

e This is a clearly expressed answer, outlining the main routes by which a slowdown impacts on the fiscal deficit.

(b) A slowdown in the performance of the German economy will adversely affect the UK in a number of ways. As incomes grow less quickly, so will the German demand for UK exports. Germany is part of the euro-zone: the relatively superior performance of the UK may drive up the value of sterling against the euro. This will also tend to make our exports less price competitive, so further reducing UK aggregate demand.

There are also likely to be wealth effects as the UK stock market is influenced by lower growth rates in the euro-zone. Confidence too is likely to be affected adversely. These reductions in UK aggregate demand will then have multiplier repercussions. **4/10 marks**

e This is a reasonable outline of the main consequences of lower growth in Germany. However, the answer has a major weakness in that it fails to address the 'assess' keyword. Some evaluative material is essential here: for example, the extent of the income effect depends on the income elasticity of demand for imports in Germany. What is happening in the rest of the euro-zone? Are other things equal in the UK? A further weakness of the answer is that no aggregate demand and supply analysis is presented.

(c) The Stability and Growth Pact was agreed by the member countries of the euro-zone as a natural follow-on to the convergence criteria imposed for initial membership of the euro. A common currency zone can only have one central bank, responsible for setting interest rates and, in this case, keeping inflation below 2%. It is therefore important that all countries have similar macroeconomic conditions, so that changes in interest rates do not adversely affect particular countries.

It is also critical that no individual country threatens the interest-setting powers of the ECB. If any member governments had too great a deficit, they would have to raise the interest rate they offered on gilts to attract funds. This would cause rates in Europe to rise generally and would undermine the autonomy of the ECB.

For these reasons the Stability and Growth Pact limits the amount of government borrowing allowed for any member state to 3% of GDP and limits the national debt to 60% of GDP.

Unfortunately, whilst this produces monetary stability it leaves the burden of adjustment to shocks to the real economy. Inevitably not all shocks hit all economies equally (e.g. the effect of an oil price rise depends on the country's trade balance in oil) whilst a single interest rate change for the whole of the euro-zone and very limited country-specific fiscal adjustment is allowed. This goes some way to explaining the problems of Germany discussed in Extract 1 and why the rules of the Stability Pact are already being broken. **8/10 marks**

e This answer contains a clear explanation of why the pact was introduced and also evaluates its significance for euro-zone stability.

(d) The 'golden rule' has been a key part of the Labour government's fiscal policy since 1997. The rule states that, on average over the business cycle, the fiscal deficit must not exceed that required to finance net public sector investment. It is therefore permissible for the government to run up counter-cyclical deficits during a recession and surpluses during strong growth, but these must cancel out and leave no underlying structural deficit. The exception is public sector investment, i.e. expenditure on bridges, new hospitals etc. The reasoning is that these provide benefits to future generations, so it is fair to borrow money from the future to finance them.

The idea behind the golden rule is to allow the government considerable medium-term flexibility in the conduct of fiscal policy. In 2002, Gordon Brown was able to present fiscal plans that involved very large increases in expenditure despite subdued growth rates. More rigid rules for fiscal policy would not have allowed the increases in health service and education expenditure that were seen to be necessary. However, this flexibility is also a disadvantage: no one can be sure when the business cycle will be complete — this can allow some slippage in fiscal restraint.

On the other hand, in a world of very low inflation rates and fixed-rule monetary policy, some form of fiscal rule is probably necessary — any structural deficit tends to accumulate rapidly in real terms if it cannot, as so often in the past, be eroded by inflation.   **10/10 marks**

> *e* This is a strongly evaluative answer that provides a clear definition of the 'golden rule' and discusses its pros and cons.

(e) Economic theory suggests that inflation rates should harmonise throughout the euro-zone. With a common currency and free trade, price differences between countries should be traded away. If the ECB keeps control of the euro money supply, there should then be every prospect of low inflation throughout the euro-zone. However, information failures may prevent this 'arbitrage' — allowing the cost of living to diverge in different parts of Europe.

The difference in monetary arrangements between the UK and the euro-zone is also significant. The MPC has had a strong record of keeping to its inflation target and can be more pragmatic about growth than the ECB. Many have criticised the ECB's terms of reference of keeping inflation below 2% as involving a deflationary bias.

A great deal depends on whether the MPC will be allowed to maintain its independence in more troubled times than it has had to deal with to date. Moving from sterling to the euro prevents hard-up governments printing money once and for all.

A major issue is that many economists argue that the euro-zone is a common currency zone large enough to withstand speculative attacks — less risk of sudden depreciation and therefore inflation. However, since the creation of the euro it is sterling that has remained strong, not the euro.

A minor issue is that it is now generally agreed that prices rose in the euro-zone countries as the euro was created — with retailers taking advantage of the confusion to raise prices, e.g. rounding up to whole euros. However, this was only a one-off price hike, so a very small contribution to overall inflation.   **7/10 marks**

> *e* This has the makings of an excellent answer, even though the candidate under pressure of time is resorting to a more 'bullet-point' approach. For full marks the answer would need a final paragraph prioritising the main issues discussed.

Total scored: 39/50 = grade A

Question 3

Trade and the global economy

Extract 1: Towards a truly open global economy

One year after ministers from more than 140 countries launched a world trade round in Doha, the threads binding together the world trading system are under strain. Despite the ministers' pledges then to create a more seamless global economy through multilateral trade deals, many are now rushing ahead with bilateral plans that could instead turn it into a patchwork quilt.

In capitals as far apart as Washington, Canberra, Singapore and Tokyo, a race is on to forge separate free trade agreements (FTAs) with countries sometimes thousands of miles away. More than 20 sets of talks have been proposed or initiated since the summer — and more are on the way.

The trend has sparked heated controversy. Countries involved in FTAs insist that removing barriers to trade and investment between them will benefit their own economies and promote broader liberalisation, strengthening the underpinnings of the World Trade Organisation (WTO) and its multilateral rules. Robert Zoellick, US trade representative, who aims to conclude FTAs with countries in Africa, Asia and the Americas, says they will trigger a beneficial process of 'competitive liberalisation', as nations vie to open their markets to each other.

Many economists and some policy-makers strongly disagree. They say bilateral deals are dangerous distractions from multilateral negotiations and a less effective route to liberalisation. Bilateralism, they claim, threatens to distort markets, create bureaucracy and business costs, and divide the world into rival economic blocs. This month the WTO director-general warned members that 'by discriminating against third countries and creating a complex network of trade regimes, such agreements pose systemic risk to the global trading system'.

One of the biggest challenges facing future FTAs is how to deal with agriculture, the last great bastion of protectionism. Many exporters believe it is much more likely to be cracked through multilateral negotiations, in which countries can trade off concessions for bigger gains, than at the bilateral level.

Meanwhile, protectionism in other areas of the world economy is by no means dead. Among industrialised countries, the USA imposes steep tariffs on imports such as clothing and footwear, which are fiercely defended by powerful producer lobbies. In many developing countries, such as India, tariffs are even higher. Some developing countries lack even permanent representation in the WTO. With the Doha round already facing tough challenges — and its end-2004 deadline looking increasingly hard to attain — some countries may decide to concentrate their energy on smaller deals that offer the prospect of more immediate results.

Source: *Financial Times*, 19 November 2002.

data-response question 3

(a) (i) Explain, giving examples, the difference between a free trade area and a customs union. (4 marks)

   (ii) Explain why agricultural subsidies are seen as a form of protectionism. (4 marks)

(b) Assess the likely benefits to a country of joining a customs union. (10 marks)

(c) Evaluate the likely welfare losses of a country imposing a quota as opposed to a tariff on imports of clothing. (10 marks)

(d) To what extent does the growth of trading blocs threaten the future growth of world trade? (10 marks)

(e) Evaluate the role of the WTO in promoting the growth of world trade. (12 marks)

■ ■ ■

Candidate's answer

(a) (i) A free trade area is an agreement between countries to abolish tariffs, quotas and other barriers to trade between them. A customs union is also a free trade area, but the member countries impose a common tariff on imports from outside the bloc. **2/4 marks**

e This answer illustrates the importance of reading the question carefully — the candidate has failed to give examples. An example of a customs union is the EU. NAFTA is a free trade area made up of Canada, the USA and Mexico.

(ii) Protectionism is any government measure designed to make it more difficult for foreign producers to gain access to domestic markets or to make it easier for domestic exporters to gain access to foreign markets. Agricultural subsidies, as favoured by both the EU and the USA, make it much more difficult for foreign producers to compete on price. They may also make exports more 'competitive' in world markets. As such, they distort market forces and limit trade based on differences in comparative costs. **4/4 marks**

e This answer defines protectionism, and then gives a clear analysis of why agricultural subsidies limit international trade.

(b) Joining a customs union will have costs as well as benefits for the country concerned. Suppose that the country had initially traded with countries outside the customs union on the basis of differences in opportunity costs. When the country joins the customs union it will have to apply the common external tariff to the imports of its former trading partners. This will probably mean that it now switches its imports to countries inside the union — buying at higher cost than before. This trade diversion will reduce consumer surplus.

However, on the other hand, all forms of existing protectionism between the country and other members of the customs union are abolished as it joins the union. This will create trade which was previously inhibited by tariffs or quotas. In the UK's case a great deal of trade creation occurred when it joined the EU — although traditional markets with non-EU countries such as New Zealand butter were adversely affected. **7/10 marks** e This is a very focused answer. It would, perhaps, have been useful to illustrate the gains from trade creation with a diagram.

(c) The imposition of a quota is generally thought to be equivalent to the imposition of a tariff. The diagram below shows a country producing at Q_H before a tariff is introduced. Demand is at Q_1 and price at P_W — the country is assumed to be small relative to the world market and so is a price taker. The tariff raises the price to P_T and reduces consumer surplus by A + B + C + D. Producer surplus rises by area A as domestic production increases to Q_S. Demand falls to Q_2 as the tariff raises the market price. Crucially, with imports of $Q_2 - Q_S$ the government receives tax revenue of area C, which it can spend on welfare-enhancing causes. The tariff results in a deadweight loss of areas B + D.

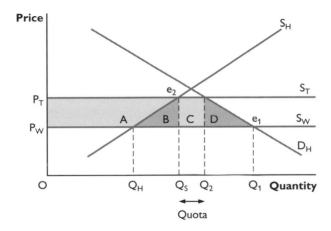

Tariffs versus quotas

However, compare this with a quota which reduces total imports to $Q_2 - Q_S$, i.e. resulting in the same amount of trade as the tariff discussed above. Although there is no tax, the limit on supply will raise the market price to P_T at equilibrium e_2. Once again, domestic output rises to Q_S. There is the same loss of consumer surplus as with the tariff (A + B + C + D). However, unlike the tariff, a quota generates no revenue for the government. Instead, a few consumers will be able to purchase $Q_2 - Q_S$ imports at the world price of P_W, so regaining consumer surplus area C. There is the same net loss to society of B+D but there are different distributional consequences. Much depends on how the quota is allocated — there are a number of possibilities, e.g. first-come-first-served, or by ballot. If the government auctions the quota it can expect to get back area C — making the impact of the quota precisely equal to that of a tariff. However, this analysis rests on the assumption that the country is small relative to world markets — not very accurate in the case of the USA's demand for clothing. **10/10 marks**

e This is a good answer based on a clear diagram and analysis of the different impact of tariffs and quotas.

(d) On the one hand, trading blocs encourage trade within them. Countries inside a customs union can see very large increases in trade as protectionism between members of the union is dismantled. Although tariffs will be reduced immediately, less visible forms of protectionism take time to remove, so the gains are not immediate.

On the other hand, trading blocs employ a variety of protectionist devices to discourage trade between blocs.

Developing countries too — many of which, like India, have very high tariffs — are forming trading blocs to counter the hegemony of developed blocs.

5/10 marks

This is only a grade-C response. The answer lacks examples to illustrate the points being made. The candidate should have made use of some case study material here, such as the 'banana wars' referred to in the Content Guidance section of this book. Disputes between the EU and the USA are rich material when answering questions of this kind.

(e) The WTO (World Trade Organisation) was established to organise the rolling conference of member countries of the GATT — convened in a series of 'rounds' to reduce protectionism, especially tariffs. Each round has achieved a significant reduction in protectionism, using the 'most favoured nation' rule that any reduction is multilateral: that is, must apply to all members. The current Doha round is looking to achieve further reductions in agricultural subsidies and to enrol developing countries in the objective of free trade.

However, the WTO is really only a convenor of conferences. It is up to the member states to make deals. As the extract suggests, these are often achieved bilaterally rather than multilaterally.

In addition, there were, from the start, exceptions to the GATT rules which allowed regional agreements rather than global ones. This has seen the rise of customs unions and free trade areas rather than a globally level playing field.

Countries tend to make multilateral agreements when, and only when, it is in their specific interests to do so. When the world economy is in recession — as at present — it becomes much more difficult to achieve reductions in protectionism.

It is also the case that some major countries were excluded for too long, e.g. China. Some have still not been admitted, e.g. Russia. This has limited the effectiveness of the WTO.

8/12 marks

This is an effective answer with a great deal of evaluation. Again, if time is available, try to produce some form of brief conclusion.

Total scored: 36/50 = grade A. This was a competent performance by a well-prepared candidate. The weaknesses in some sections were compensated for by a very strong answer on the welfare effects of tariffs and quotas.